The Mutt Styling Guide

Chrissy Thompson

Illustrations by Denise Benko

AARONCO Pet Products, Inc.
248 West Old Country Road
Hicksville, NY 11801
www.aaroncopet.com

Published in 2005 by AARONCO Pet Products, Inc.

ISBN 0-9646072-8-X

Manufactured in the United States of America

Illustrations by Denise Benko

Cover Photograph by:
Steve Grubman Photography, Inc.
456 North Morgan
Chicago, IL 60622

OTHER BOOKS BY AARONCO

The All Breed Dog Grooming Guide
All About Dog Shows
Boarding Kennel Management
The Cat Grooming Guide
The Business Guide to Pet Grooming

Acknowledgments

There are so many friends (people and dogs) to thank for helping me to, "Keep On, Keepin' On!" in this wonderful new adventure.

First and always foremost is my terrific husband, Rick (there just aren't enough superlatives) and of course Joe, the best "Mutt" in the whole world! The two of you not only put up with me at home and work but constantly inspired and encouraged me not to mention loved me when I was unlovable . . . Thank You!

Whenever I would need an extra ounce of strength to continue on, I would call Rachel Pelone, The best Mother-in-law I could ever ask for. Thank you Rachel, for always being there when I need you.

Thank you Denise Benko, the angel who came into my life, pencil in hand and talent overflowing. This book never would have been accomplished without you. You are a wonderful artist and I'm proud to work with you. Thank you for all the love and friendship.

Thank you Joyce Carter, my wonderful new aunt, for the many, "You Go Get 'Em Girls!" you were always providing.

Many thanks to Linda Essman and "Little Sophie" for not only editing but encouraging and being a wealth of knowledge. What great friends!

I also want to thank Vicki England Patton, my final editor. Thank you for your help, unending knowledge and patience.

There are a lot of people in the "Dog World" to whom I am so appreciative of their support and wisdom that I can't begin to list them. Please know how grateful I am. The three people to whom I will be forever indebted are Sam and Cynthia Kohl and Sam Radmin. Not only did they take a chance publishing a newcomer but they lovingly guided me through rough spots and their unending knowledge has not just made "The Mutt Styling Guide" grow up and mature but they have also become dear friends. Thank You All!!!

Gratefully,

Chrissy Thompson

Dedication

I dedicate this book to my loving husband, Rick, who has continuously been by my side helping me, but most importantly for believing in me. This book is as much his as it is mine.

"Love is eternal." Corinthians 13:8

About the Author

I have the very best job in the whole world—professional dog groomer! I started grooming dogs over twenty-five years ago when my children were four years old and five months old and I needed to make money while I was home with them.

At the time, I owned a Miniature Schnauzer, named Samantha and had been taking her for what I thought was professional grooming. After her appointments, Samantha was usually shaved bald, her little cropped Schnauzer ears nicked on their edges and her skin flaky. I was never satisfied with the results and the thought came to me, "I bet I could do a better job myself!"

It took a couple of months of persistent questioning to find out where and how to start learning this trade. Remember, there were no personal computers and no Internet at the time—but I was determined! After all, I loved dogs so how bad could working with them be?

I asked Norma, my dog groomer, for direction in pursuing this crazy idea, but she was no help. Back in the Dark Ages of dog grooming, groomers did not share information about the trade for fear of losing their clientele to new, up and coming competitors. Even today, it is still very difficult to persuade many dog groomers to share fresh ideas learned from their personal experiences, but thankfully we are beginning to see changes in this myopic attitude. With the millions of dogs in the United States alone, there is certainly enough business for us all!

Tenacity became the name of the game. Finally, Norma, who refused to teach me herself, put me in touch with Sheila, a groomer who agreed to train me. After paying her a whopping $200, I was on my way!

Sheila's grooming shop was a sight to behold—a small dark section of her basement with just enough room for two people, a few ticks and a dog! It was so dark that if you moved away from the grooming table, you had no idea where you were. The dogs were bathed in a cement laundry tub. Because it was divided down the middle into two sections, it was very difficult to fit some dogs in it, needing to either scrunch the dog into one side or to have the unfortunate larger dogs straddle the middle divider. Very awkward to say the least!

We had two sets of clippers. The first set was a one speed model onto which you would simply snap your blades into place, but the other set was definitely more of a challenge. To change the blade on this A-2 clipper the head had to be screwed on and off with a screwdriver! There were only skip-tooth clipper blades and only in sizes #7, #5, and #4. We thought we had died and gone to heaven when someone invented the finishing blades!

Sheila had only two pairs of scissors and I wasn't taught anything about thinning shears, curved scissors, bent-shank scissors, or scissors with any other size blade but an 8". Talk about scary, it was so long, to me it looked like the length of a football field.

Back then we charged clients eight dollars for Miniature Schnauzers, ten dollars for Toy and Miniature Poodles, and twelve dollars for Cocker Spaniels.

I trained with Sheila for six months. The last two of those months consisted of Sheila sitting in her kitchen with the girls, drinking coffee! After essentially grooming on my own those last two months, I thought I had learned enough and asked myself the big question: "Am I ready to start my own dog grooming business now?" The answer was: "I was wondering when you'd get around to asking that question!" So, with that mental "graduation ceremony," my training with Sheila was over and I was out the door, off to begin my new career!

After twenty-five years, give or take, I now have Chrissy's Paw Spa. I can honestly tell you that I love this job as much today as I did when I groomed my very first dog all those years ago, because as my husband, Rick tells people, it is because I have a passionate love for what I do. He is absolutely right.

About the Artist

Writing a book is a complex process, and not an easy task, especially for the first-time author. However, writing the words was only half the battle. Figuring out how to visually present my thoughts and ideas was the other half. My artistic ability lies in grooming dogs, not in creating illustrations for a book.

So, after pondering the problem of what kind of visuals to use to demonstrate my ideas, I ruled out photographs because I wanted to take the same dog and put different styles on it – like changing outfits on a doll—a nearly impossible task using photographs. Drawings then were the only way to show you my vision of magnificently groomed mutts. That left me with the task of finding an artist who was good enough to get into my head and then be able to draw what was found there.

My friend J.T. knows all sorts of people and she introduced me to a friend of hers who is an art teacher and she thought we'd work well together. Enter Denise Benko. Thank you, J.T., you were absolutely correct!

Denise and I hit it off right away. In fact, I can honestly say I knew she was perfect right from the start. She's such a talented lady and fun to work with. Denise is blessed with an ability to listen, absorb, and interpret artistically in a way that is truly uncanny. She was able to get into my head and draw what was found there. Denise has just as much passion for her art as I do for my grooming, which makes us a dynamite team.

Not only do I own a dog and cat grooming shop but I also own three large dogs, the smallest of which weighs 85 pounds. My dogs, and some of the dogs groomed in my shop, acted as models for the illustrations in this book. Although Denise loves animals, she is highly allergic to cats and dogs.

With this very large problem, we ended up having to meet at "safe" places such as restaurants or coffee shops to keep her from suffering severe allergy attacks. But if she needed to see one of the dogs in person, she would load up on her allergy medication and get in and out of the shop as quickly as possible.

Her intense participation on this project turned her home studio into what her husband and two sons have dubbed, "Mom's Kennel." Now if that isn't love and dedication, I sure don't know what is!

Denise and I felt that for you to successfully groom these mutts, you need to stand back and smile, laugh and enjoy them too, as we do. Denise will draw these cute little guys in different styles so you can envision and see beyond the scruffy little dog at your feet, and I will describe how to accomplish these feats.

Contents

Contents (cont.d)

Foreword

There isn't a groomer in business anywhere on earth that has not been faced with having to transform a nondescript bundle of fur into a vision of loveliness. Underlying even the homeliest mutt is a potentially beautiful dog just waiting to be revealed. All too often, when facing the challenge of making over the average mutt, the groomer will quickly decide he/she is dealing with a dog where nothing can be done to enhance its looks and the only choice is to just bathe the dog and leave it at that.

Chrissy Thompson has solved the riddle of not only making over the mutts that come to you for beauty help, she teaches you to study each dog and decide which particular breeds are dominant in each dog's appearance. She then shows you what can be accomplished in transforming the dog into the breed it most closely resembles. She not only gives you different examples of what can be done to improve the looks of each dog, she tells you how to do it. There are many times that a groomer has saved a poor little mutt's life by enhancing its looks and making it appealing enough to be adopted. In addition to making your customer happy, there is the added advantage of increasing your income by being paid for a complete grooming instead of a mere fee for a dog's bath.

Follow Chrissy's instructions and you will grow your business and keep it growing for years to come.

Sam Kohl

Chapter One

Mutt Grooming—Getting Started

Dog Grooming: We're An Industry Now!

Grooming dogs is no longer a backyard or basement endeavor. We've come a long way! It is a **profession** and we are **professionals**. We are educated and we are artists. Groomers are a certain breed and not just anyone can do what we do. Be proud—I am!

There are many ways to acquire information to keep improving ourselves as groomers and business people. The first and most obvious choice for acquiring knowledge is to attend one of the dog grooming schools that are around the country. Years ago, grooming schools were in their infancy and rather primitive. Schools now are greatly improved. Do your homework to find a really good one as close to you as possible.

You can access the Internet for grooming and breed information available on various websites. You can go into chat rooms and confer with other groomers. You can subscribe to email newsletters and newsgroups. You can find and shop for grooming supplies and products online. The internet is a vast resource for the dog grooming professional. Use it.

A thrilling way to learn more is to attend one of the many grooming seminars given frequently throughout the country. In this way, you get the chance to talk face to face with other groomers and meet trade people who will be happy to demonstrate new equipment innovations and new supplies especially designed for groomers. The grooming competitions at these seminars are great fun for the contestants as well as the audience. I highly recommend them!

Take any opportunity to see or attend dog shows. The television commentators are a wealth of information about dog history and new breeds now being recognized by the Kennel Clubs. If you are watching a dog show broadcast on television, make sure to pay attention to the commercials too. You'll get an update on new products and some breed information thrown in too.

Another way to learn is to read grooming-related books. Buy those you like a lot and find most useful. Every shop needs easily accessible reference books if only to check on details of different breeds and their styles during a grooming. The bible of dog grooming guides is Sam Kohl's, "The All Breed Dog Grooming Guide." It's up-to-date and groomer friendly. I also get a lot of information out of the many dog magazines on the market and some of the best known names in the industry have made videos. What a great way to learn from the best!

We are so fortunate to be in the grooming profession now because things are rapidly and continually changing for the better. However, our trade does not require groomers to be licensed. Currently it is not required nationwide and may never be but as professionals we need to begin to think in terms of standards for our industry. This will not only be good for us but for our clients too. They expect their pets to get the best of care, and rightfully so. They expect us to treat their dogs as we would treat our own and to know our jobs inside and out. Groomers also act as their link to breed information, veterinarians, products, parasites, and general dog knowledge. Licensing would require groomers to meet minimum standards set by the industy, require continuing education, and improve the level of performance of groomers everywhere.

Remember, you will not appear like a well informed professional if you don't have the knowledge, so always strive to keep as current as possible. Do your best to keep up to date, and one step ahead of your clients when it comes to the subject of dogs. I always have at least one book about dogs that I am currently reading, whether it is about grooming, breed information and standards, massage therapy for dogs, pet communication, health or training techniques. If you need a change, you can always read about people skills and business techniques. When you are in this state of mind, I highly recommend Dale Carnegie's "How to Win Friends and Influence People." There is always room for improvement for yourself and the industry.

Another area within the grooming world that is constantly improving is the area of equipment development. There are so many innovative people in our industry who develop new products and equipment that not only make our jobs easier, but also safer and more professional.

We now have ergonomic equipment, air purifiers, clipper vacuuming systems and even something as simple as good pairs of scissors for left handed people that can make us so much more produc-

4

tive and comfortable at the same time. I take my hat off to these innovators of our industry.

Another possible avenue for you to explore in this industry is your creative side, to come up with new and different grooming products. Do you have a good idea? All it takes is a good concept and the tenacity to make it happen. Remain open-minded and use your imagination. Remember, if you can see a need for a new product or tool, thousands of your fellow groomers have the very same need. It's a market waiting to be filled.

There is such importance in appearance and looking the part. I recently attended a grooming seminar in Charlotte, North Carolina and was amazed to see one of the groomers attending the seminar wearing plum colored sweat pants with a big hole in the fanny. Appalling as it may seem, its not the first time I'd seen this kind of thing. Now, just imagine being a client and seeing your groomer for the first time. The first impression a client gets is so important and you only get one chance at making it a good one. If you are dressed in a clean neat uniform or smock and are happy to see the client and their dog, the client will feel comfortable leaving their pet in your care. I recommend that groomers wear a uniform because they look best and are easy to maintain. If you, yourself, do not have a clean, neat appearance, why would anyone leave their dog with you to be cleaned up and looking good?

Another good first impression comes about with that initial telephone contact with the prospective client. Before you answer the phone, remember to smile and think to yourself: this is the best job in the whole world. You must be able to project your enthusiasm and professionalism from the first moment.

The Mutt Grooming Toolbox

Earlier, I was telling you about equipment I never knew existed when I was a beginner. Today, however, groomers have cutting edge products available which are designed specifically for faster, safer and more precise grooming. I'm going to list some of the tools that I use and you can adapt what you have in your grooming tool box or add to it if you're missing some of these items. Because this book is written for the professional groomer, I'll assume you do not need instructions on their proper use.

Clippers & Blades

When choosing your clipper, pick up and handle the different types and brands taking into consideration what you need. Consider their shape, weight, and whether you need corded or cordless. I keep both Andis and Oster heavy-duty two-speed electric clippers for heavier jobs. Nothing is worse than having your clipper break down in the middle of the work day and have nothing to fall back on.

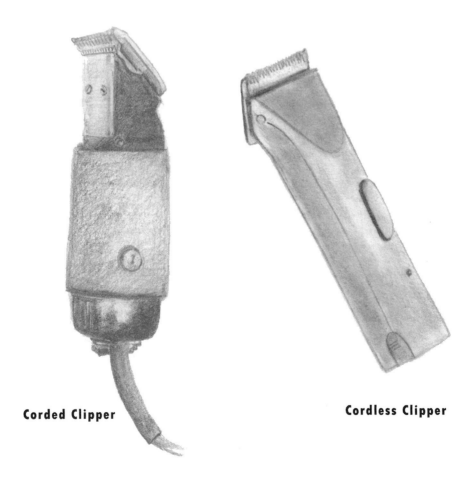

Corded Clipper

Cordless Clipper

I also added a set of small cordless Wahl Arco clippers to my toolbox. They are small and light weight and go into small, hard to get to places. The blades are unique because one blade can range to five different sizes with the flip of a switch.

There are many clipper blade sizes to choose from. Fortunately, the length and sizing of the different manufacturer's blades are uniform and range from the larger the number having the closest and shortest cut to the smaller numbers leaving more hair. I keep size #40 and #30 blades to use under snap on combs. The #15 and #10

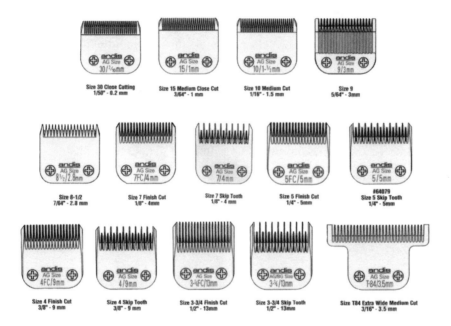

blades I use on rectum and groin areas, inside ears and on faces, some patterns—depending on how short the client wants the style, and for clipping out some stubborn matting. I also keep #7, #5, and #4 blades in both skip tooth and finishing styles. They leave the hair longer but still short enough to be easier to care for. The last blade I keep on hand is the #5/8" blade. These make it easy to get into close, tight places such as hard tight matting between the dog's pads.

Uniformity of sizes between manufacturers does not carry through when it comes to snap on combs. The best thing to do is to start out with the biggest comb and work the sizes down to the length you desire. I use snap on combs as a shortcut to take off the bulk of the coat and finish by evening with my scissors.

Snap On Combs

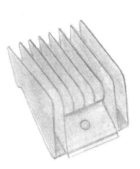

Clipper Vacuuming System

By far, my most favorite piece of equipment is my clipper vacuuming system. This device attaches to your clipper and sucks the cut coat into a container as you are clipping. Not only does it reduce your grooming and clean-up time, it is also healthier because it prevents loose hair, dirt and dander from flying into the air. There are several different manufacturers for these systems, so do your homework to find the one that will most closely meet your personal needs.

I bought my first clipper vacuuming system for my shop in 1995. I had seen it demonstrated many times at grooming seminars and had talked myself out of buying it with all my many good reasons. Top of the list was that it scared me to death! Also, I thought it was too expensive, too heavy, and too awkward. I knew that groomers never needed this device before, so "if the system ain't broke, don't fix it!" Okay, wrong again.

But with all my justifications not to get one of these machines, I could not get it out of my mind. I had to have one. Now, all I had to do was convince the three other groomers who worked at my shop, to attach this gadget to their clippers. Using a little diplomacy, threats of job loss, and insisting they try it for themselves, they were thrilled too! So I had a four-station system installed and now I don't know how I ever managed without it for all those years. If you don't have one, get one! It's one of the best investments you can make.

Scissors

I have a whole tray of scissors that are good ones, but I don't use them all because scissors are a very personal thing. Scissors are an extension of your own hand and your choice of scissor depends on what works best for you. They do what you think them to do. I prefer to use smaller, lighter weight scissors. They are easier on the wrists and allow me to get into smaller areas.

One of my groomers, says that I use my scissors faster than she can use her clippers. The secret to acheiving that speed is based mostly on the scissors I choose to use. Try using smaller, lightweight scissors and see if that works for you too. If it does, tell a friend.

Other scissors in my toolbox include a pair of 10" straights, 6½" curved, 6" thinning shears, and a 4" straight with pointed tips.

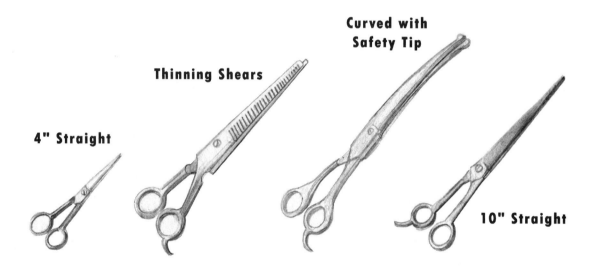

Curved with Safety Tip

Thinning Shears

4" Straight

10" Straight

It's well worth the extra money to invest in really good expensive scissors, once you find out which styles you like best and are the most comfortable to use. I purchased my favorite thinning shears three years ago and they were costly. However, they've never once had to be sharpened in all this time. This isn't because they aren't loved and used constantly, but because of the high quality of the metal and the craftsmanship that went into making them. I use them for blending, shaping and shortening.

Because scissors can be expensive investments, especially if you buy several of the same pair as back-ups, I strongly recommend you go out of your way to protect them. Though made of metal, they are not indestructable, and their cutting ability can become compromised if they are not taken care of properly. I use a leather pouch to store my scissors in, always keeping them safe and away from moisture when they're not in use.

Leather Pouch

Combs & Brushes

Combs are just as important as brushes and there are almost as many styles. They can have handles or no handles—use those that are the most comfortable for you. When referring to combs, coarse, medium and fine refer to the size of the teeth and how close or far apart they are placed—coarse being large and spaced far apart, and fine being small and placed closely together.

I have several combs that I particularly like and I especially prefer the new teflon coated combs that help reduce static electricity. I have a 7¼" coarse comb I use to fluff out Bichons and Poodles. My most used comb is the 7¼" Fine to Coarse Tooth Comb which I use after brushing the dog. This comb makes sure I didn't miss any hidden matting.

Metal Comb

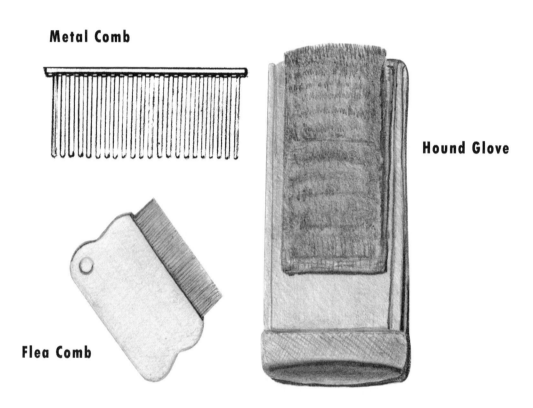

Hound Glove

Flea Comb

For combing around a dog's eyes I use either a 4" Fine to Medium Comb or a Flea Comb, preferring the style with a single row of teeth and a handle.

When it comes to brushes, I use a large and a medium sized slicker brush with hard (coarse) pins which I use on bigger dogs having tougher skin and a coarser coat. I also have a medium and a smaller sized slicker brush with soft (fine) pins to use on the smaller more delicate skinned dogs. I use a wooden handled Pin Brush on long full coated breeds because it helps protect the hair against breakage.

Last, but not least, I use a hound glove with natural bristles to help release the coat oils, loose hair, dirt, and flakey skin on short coated dogs.

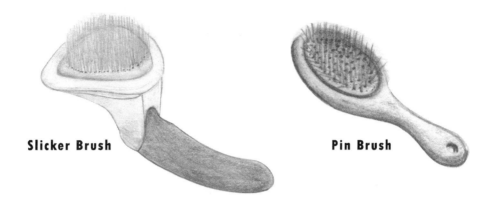

Slicker Brush   **Pin Brush**

Nail Trimmers

There are a variety of types: The scissors-type for small nails, the guillotine-type for medium sized nails, and the pliers-type which are found in assorted sizes. Pliers-type trimmers are more versatile because they are open on the end.

Nail Clipper

Other Tools & Tricks

I also keep a coarse stripping knife and shedding blade for removing dead undercoat, a pair of straight Hairmostats® for removing ear hair, putting in bows and tick removal. In addition I also keep my V Rake® which I use for dematting when I want to save as much of the dog's coat as I can.

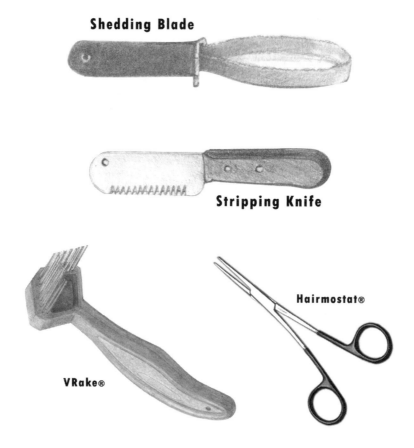

Shedding Blade

Stripping Knife

VRake®

Hairmostat®

Other items used in creating your finished product—the best looking dog—are latex bands for topknots, pigtails and bows. I use larger flat ones for topknots and pigtails because they do not mat as fast and do not slide out easily. I use smaller ones when making bows because they can twist up tighter and faster and a smaller section of hair is used to slip it onto. This elminates the possibility of matting and it also stays put better. Latex bands now come in colors too, so be creative.

To make your own bows, loop approximately 4" of ribbon. Take the center of the loop at the top and pinch it down behind the crossover. Wrap a small latex band several times around the center pinched section until it's tightly secured. Be as creative as you wish by adding nylon net, ribbon roses, a second bow, or streamers.

Making A Bow

Bandanas can be bought premade, but a less expensive way is to make your own. If you buy the fabric in bolts of three yards there will be very little waste. Lay the material out flat with the fold on the right side. Take hold of the corners on the cut bottom edge and fold it over to the open edges on your left. You have just formed a triangle. With pinking shears, cut across the top edge of the triangle through all four layers. Fold the triangle in half and cut the new fold. Open the cut triangle and you will have four large bandanas. To make these large bandanas smaller keep folding the triangles in half and cut the new fold until you get the size you need. The three yard piece of material will provide approximately twenty large bandanas.

It's also a good idea to keep baby wipes on hand to wipe out the dog's ears, doggie mouth wash to freshen their breath, and cologne scented the same as the shampoo and conditioner used on the dog.

Ergonomics

Make sure you investigate the new ergonomic equipment on the market. I cannot stress this enough: Take care of your body! It too is part of your livelihood and more important than any other piece of equipment in your toolbox because you only get one. Wear good shoes and use rubber matting to stand on. This will help protect your feet, ankles, knees, and hips from repetitive damage caused by impact with hard flooring surfaces. If you need more support anywhere, get wrist, back, knee, or elbow braces, use the new comfort-grip equipment, etc. If you can afford a hydraulic grooming table: Get One! If not, there are leg extensions for regular grooming tables available for taller people. There are so many more items than there were when I started grooming in that dark basement all those years ago, many of which will help you take better care of your body. To discover what new products become available that will make your job easier, faster, and might reduce occupational injuries, make it a quarterly task to page through grooming supply catalogs.

Assessing the Challenge In Front Of You

At least a quarter of all the grooming challenges that come into my shop are of that elusive breed known as the "mutt," so where does that leave us? No two mixes are the same. Each mutt has unique styling requirements which makes grooming them an interesting artistic challenge but also downright scary because groomers have never been taught what can be done with a mutt, even though you may have gone to school or apprenticed.

You know how to groom the traditional purebreeds such as the Poodle, Schnauzer, and the Cocker Spaniel, among others. But what to do with a dog that has no known ancestral lines? When I first started grooming twenty-five years ago, we didn't know anything about styling. The thought of mutts, or dogs of mixed breeds, coming in for a grooming was terrifying because who knew what to do with them? But, I did what everyone else does when in doubt. I avoided them, and in the process, missed out on an additional source of income and the chance to grow my business. I don't recommend you take this road!

As a groomer, a prospective client may describe their dogs to you as having "no known origin." It is your job to guide the client, but most groomers have no idea where to begin because no one has taken on the task of teaching us grooming for mutts. This section will instruct you on what factors to take into account when deciding what to do when a new mutt enters your shop. Follow these five steps when evaluating a dog on its first visit and you'll be well on your way to turning this furry diamond in the rough into a gemstone.

Take a deep breath and don't panic! See it as a creative challenge, an opportunity to grow your business, and a chance to show off your professionalism. The one thing that we know for sure about mutts, mongrels and mixed breeds is that they are loved as much as the pure breeds and their owners want them to look as good as a show dog just before competition.

First Visit Evaluation

Imagine this all too likely scenario! You get a phone call from a prospective client who declares her dog is a mutt, who we'll call Chester. Do you take the appointment? Well, yes, but first you need to get more information.

Step One: While you are still on the telephone with Chester's owner, ask her the following question, "If you had to pick a breed that your dog looks the most like, what would it be?" If this gets you nowhere, with a response like "just a hairy dog," you will need to at least ascertain its general size so you can plan cage space, approximate grooming and drying time, or if Chester even needs a full styling. Ask the owner about Chester's physical problems, and coat length and type. All this will help you in planning what you do next.

Step Two: Appointment day arrives and you meet Chester for the first time. Be aware that this is a crucial time because you need to talk to both canine and client at the same time, gathering information from them both. While I'm talking to Chester's owner, I'm usually kneeling down and at eye level with Chester. This puts me in a nonaggressive position and Chester does not feel threatened as he might if I were looming over him. *Do not* take Chester out of his owner's arms because he may feel this is an aggressive move toward her and he might try to protect her. She needs to put him on the floor. This helps me gain Chester's confidence because curiosity has gotten the best of him and he is probably coming up to me without a fuss. *Tip: Have some chewing gum or candy in your mouth. The smell is a good attention getter.*

At this point I am also starting to evaluate Chester's disposition. How much will he put up with? Is he fearful, aggressive, or the typical, easygoing sort? If he will not come up to me, I will take hold of the lead—for safety reasons no dog should be off lead in the shop.

While you are gaining Chester's owner's confidence and winning her trust, you need to project that you not only care about her dog but you also care about her feelings, too. In today's world, it's so hard to find someone who will listen with respect, so you must learn to be in charge but do it diplomatically. If she is asking you to do the impossible or in some cases, insisting, steer her in the right direction without being pushy or a know-it-all. If she should want you to do the impossible demat for instance, tell her how painful it would be to Chester. Tell her that you know that she doesn't want this and neither do you. It's cruel. By including her in the decision you give her part of the responsibility, "We can take him down (don't use the word shave) this time so we can get started growing him back out. In a few weeks, he'll look like a puppy again."

Now is the time to stress to her that no one should laugh at him. It will hurt his feelings and he may hide, become depressed or even get snappy. How would she feel? This will show her how much you care about Chester and yet you have still succeeded in getting your own way without making anyone feel uncomfortable. This partnership helps your business continue to grow because of your compassion for both canine and client.

Step Three: As I am asking the owner what she might have in mind for Chester's grooming, I need to look beyond this hairy creature to see a breed look or a combination of breed types. Look at each body section individually and then as a whole. What do you see? Remember that you're also listening to the owner. Listen for hidden information. "We're so busy!" This of course, means that her family doesn't have the time to brush Chester and that you need to steer her toward a nice easy utility clip or convince her that she will need to preset appointments for every week or two so you can keep him clean and brushed out as *she likes him*. Again this is putting the decision back in her court. "I love to see his eyes. They're so pretty!" She just told you to clear out the eyes and make them a focal point. "We hate getting dripped on after he gets a drink or eats." There you are! Shorten his ears and beard a lot.

Without saying it, she is clearly telling you what she wants. You just have to be perceptive and know what to listen for.

Step Four: Evaluate Chester's body. Is he overweight? Does he have eyes that seep? Are his front quarters higher than his back quarters? Is his body too long? What do I need to work around? Remember, you're being creative here and you are in the position to change the whole look by accentuating the positive and downplaying the negative. Can you make the dog look more proportional by making heavy dogs look lighter, and making skinny dogs look healthy, or, proportion dogs heads that are too large for their small bodies. You are the artist.

Step Five: Examine Chester's coat. Is it curly and coarse like a Poodle, or straight and coarse like a Lhasa Apso? Is it soft and cottony or silky? The biggest question of all, that I am trying to get answered while I am down here trying to get Chester to come up to me on his own so I can touch him is: "how matted is he?" This definitely has bearing on what styles can be tried.

It's now time for Chester's owner to leave. I'll say to Chester, "Okay. We'll stay here and watch Mom leave." This tactfully lets the owner know it's time for her to go. I always add here, "Please don't worry. I will take good care of Chester. This is like preschool for him."

With the information you've gathered during a first visit evaluation such as this one, you're now almost equipped to make styling decisions for any mutt that may walk through your shop door. Now, all we have to do is combine all this information and come up with a unique styling solution for the mutt before you.

Using the Evaluation Information To Create a Style

You've just gone through a similar first visit evaluation with one of your client's pets. What do you see after looking at the dog following these five steps? Does a certain breed's characteristics dominate in this mixed up breed of dog? Does one part of the dog resemble a certain breed, and another part of the dog resemble a different breed? Identifying possible breeds in the mutt's lineage, and recognizing a dominant breed can help guide you in creating the best style for the dog.

This is why it's so important to know your breeds. This is the key to pulling it all together. You don't have to do all one type of cut on the same dog. You may end up putting Schnauzer body and legs on Max with a Border Terrier face. Katie looks like a Wire Haired Dachshund and Terrier mix. Katie's current styling entails a #10 blade down the back, blending into the sides and legs, leaving a skirt that follows the contours of the brisket up to the tuck up of the loin and scissoring the legs into pipes. Her head is done like a Schnauzer with eyebrows and beard and I scissor her short pendulum ears to the leather. Last but not least, is her long tail. The hair is not long, so we just leave it natural. But in my mind's eye, I can envision Katie in other looks. If I were to change this grooming into something totally different, I would give Katie a Wire Haired Dachshund look, just by shaping her head with eyebrows and beard, thin her out and trim any flyaways off her body and legs.

I'm able to see these things not only because I'm an artist, but also because I know my breeds! So, how do you decide what to do with a mutt that is awaiting a new look? Before getting into actual styling of dogs and their grooming instructions, let's go through my decision making process together. The following factors help me determine what will make "mutt magic" for this dog. When you follow this process, combined with your creativity, you can create it too.

1. Breed Dominance

Look beyond the dog in front of you to see a breed look or a combination of breed types. Again, I cannot stress enough how important it is that you know the different breeds. Look at the size, shape, color, markings, and coat texture. Choose the prominent features and the breed it most resembles. The one that comes to mind first is usually the right answer.

2. Additional Breed Recognition

After looking at the dog as a whole, study each body section individually. You are specifically looking for features not necessarily of the dominant breed but one still needing to be accentuated because of their unique qualities. For instance, accent big liquid brown eyes on a small Border Terrier, Parson Russell Terrier mix who has a little Shih Tzu in him. By emphasizing each mutt's attributes whether it's a silky coat, outstanding markings, or those large entreating eyes, you will be accentuating the dog's positives and enhancing his looks.

3. Proportion Proportion Proportion

The three P's of dog grooming are Proportion, Proportion, Proportion.

Your job as the stylist is to use the dog's hair to adjust any part of his body to be relative to the rest of his body. This will give a symmetrical and harmonious illusion to his appearance. For instance, rid your dog of "toothpick legs" and a sausage-like body by cutting the coat on the body short and the hair on the legs longer, making them appear thicker.

You can make a very thin looking dog appear heavier and healthier by styling it with a longer coat to cover its boniness.

A dog with rear legs that are shorter than his front legs can become miraculously proportionate by angling the length of the coat on his back longer over the rump to shorter at the withers and shoulders. This creates the illusion of a straight back.

Now make the dog with windmill ears lose the look of being able to take off and fly by giving him a round Bichon shaped head, thus filling in the gaps with hair.

Evaluate each dog's problem areas. Use your imagination to create a solution to the problem, then all that's left to do is go ahead and fix it. You're the artist!

4. Coat Type and Texture

Types of coat and their texture is an important factor in determining the style that will be possible to create and will look the best on each individual mutt. The Cocker Spaniel's thick and long coat may be curly when it's short and wavy when it's long. You would use straight scissors to shape or shorten it. You could not get the same result from the Petit Basset Griffon Vendeen's coat which is rough and wiry. Instead of scissoring, you'll be using your fingers to pluck or your thinning shears to even any exceptionally long guard hairs that detract from the dog's appearance.

Let's compare the coat of the Bichon Frise with the Lhasa Apso. The Bichon has silky and curly hair that stands out and is sculpted with straight and curved scissors, while the Lhasa's coat is straight and more like human hair. Use a snap on comb on the clipper, thinning shears or straight scissors while shaping and shortening his coat or let it grow into full length.

Look at the Havanese with his soft and long coat. Use a snap on comb on the clipper, straight scissors or thinning shears to shorten it or let it grow out to a long full coat.

The Irish Water Spaniel's coat is totally different with its soft tight curls that are shaped and evened with scissors.

The examples above show that even though you're working on mutts, it is critical to know your breeds and their coat types and textures. A mutt can have different coat types on different parts of his body, so using your breed knowledge, separate these parts, and address each area accordingly.

5. Anatomical Anomolies

Mutts always have irregularities for us to work around. Therefore, following breed standards to guide us helps, but it does not provide a complete solution. The Question and Answer section that follows deals with quite a few challenges we're faced with but there are some more I'd like to present.

There are a few dogs that for one reason or another are blind and their eyes are unattractive or only have one eye and the other one is sealed. We want to make them as attractive as possible and if there is hair to work with we can be pretty creative. Of course, if the dog has short hair on the head, such as the German Shepherd, Golden

Retreiver, Border Terrier, etc., we as groomers can't do much about that.

If the dog has a straight coat, it will be easy to make Schnauzer or Scotty eyebrows. Eyebrows are harder to create with a wavy or curly coat so a good alternative in this case is to scissor a visor or create a fall and beard similar to a Kerry Blue Terrier's. In all of these cases, leave enough length to hide the unattractive condition you are trying to conceal.

Now, going to the other end of the spectrum, instead of hiding the eyes another way of exposing the eyes is to make a top knot or pigtails on the top of the head. The top knot doesn't necessarily have to be very long but keep it in proportion to the rest of the dog.

Have you ever been presented with a mutt with huge prick ears? One suggestion to help hide these "satellite dishes" is to give them butterfly ears. Let the hair grow off the ear like a Papillon, Skye Terrier, or Briard but the coat must be straight or only slightly wavy.

Another alternative is to partially hide those ears with coarse-hair like a West Highland White Terrier or Cairn Terrier. Make the top of the head as long as possible but keep this rule in mind, if the top of the head parts, it's too long, so trim more off. The one thing I would do differently from either of those two breeds is, I wouldn't shave the ears but scissor the ear tips to the leather. It will prevent the ears from appearing too harsh.

Now, let's reverse the problem. We can counteract drop ears that are too short. They can be made to appear longer by not only growing the ear feathering out as long as possible but by also shaving the top one-third of the ear on both sides. When measuring the top one-third use the top of the ear and the bottom of the feathering for references.

Another way to elongate drop ears is to use a modified Bedlington Terrier or Dandie Dinmont Terrier style ear. After clipping, when forming the tassle, make the bottom of the diamond as long as proportionately possible.

Now to elongate a dog's muzzle, it's pretty simple if the beard can be grown out, keeping in mind the three "P's." Then if it's still too short, try pointing the bottom like a goatee. This can really give the illusion of length.

6. Styling and the Wishes of the Client

This is probably the most important factor you should consider when deciding how to groom a mutt! You can put all your creative ideas into motion but if the client has something else in mind, more than likely they won't be happy with what you create.

Because you may not be given formal instructions, rather, the owner may make their preferences known during casual conversation, you must listen to everything that the client says to you from the beginning of your conversation.

"We take him swimming all the time." To this I usually suggest a short haircut.

Or, "Those little wisps on top of her head are her personality, don't you think?" I'm not going to cut those off for anything!

Another good one is: "I'm so sick of all the hair in my house, it's even in my refrigerator." Well, I know I'm going to make this one really short or work super hard to get every single dead hair out of its coat.

Or, "He's my baby (puppy, etc.)" In cases like this I'm going to lean toward suggesting a "cutesie" haircut.

"He's always bringing mulch and stuff from the yard into the house." I'm going to ask this person if I can take the feet as short as possible and then I'll go on to suggest shorter legs and a T-Clip.

Take your styling cues from the client's lifestyle with the dog, and their preferences regarding how the dog should look and you will ensure a happy repeat customer.

7. Is This A "Caution" Dog?

Last, but not least, you will need to consider the dog's disposition. If a dog is a "Caution Dog," one which does not cope well with the grooming process, you don't want to suggest an intricate style which will take a long time for the dog to endure. See if you can just keep it simple for your sake and for the dog's sake as well.

After reviewing these seven factors, you are now ready to decide what is the best grooming solution for this mutt. You've started along the path to making "mutt magic." Now, let's go do it.

24

Chapter Two

Creating A Unique Mutt Style
by Mixing and Matching

Meet Our Anatomy Model, Joe—He's Special

Can you relate at least one good story about each of your friends? I know I can. It's what makes them individual, not to mention special. All of my clients, whether it be the dog or the person have a specialness about them that helps me remember and relate to them.

Let me tell you about Joe. We think Joe is a mixture of Bernese Mountain Dog, Golden Retriever and maybe a little Newfoundland. A man called the shop about 11:00 AM one day. He was a shop teacher at one of the local schools and while he was teaching, his class saw this dog out in the road. Picture this, they all went out and finally caught the dog but he was a mess and needed cleaning up desperately. "Could I get him in now?" he asked. What could I say, with a background story like that, but "Sure what's one more?" Besides I've always been a sucker for a good story.

You guessed it. There is more to the story. This poor little waif was a mess. Skinny, burrs, mats, dried blood, lacerations, but worst of all was the rusty choker chain embedded in his neck. I took him in late, so of course, I groomed him and as I was gently cleaning him up, I felt I had literally jumped into the most empathetic, liquid brown eyes I had ever gazed into. "Mr. No Name" was really a person inside a dog and he was communicating with me with these wonderful eyes. I'm sure you've seen and felt that too, at one time or another.

Of course, our teacher was the last to pick up that day and "Mr. No Name", my own Newfy, Jonathan and I were the only ones there. I was busy telling this man what a terrific dog he had saved as he was handing me the check. He then proceeded to tell me he lived in an apartment and probably couldn't keep him. I told him I might be able to help him place this poor little orphan if he couldn't. That man's eyes lit up as he got the most appealing look on his face and said, "Really?"

I handed him back his check. I didn't even get it rung up in the cash register. I never was to see or hear from him again, but he blessed me with "Joe"' my very own "Angel Unaware" and next to my husband, Rick, the very best friend I have.

BODY ANATOMY

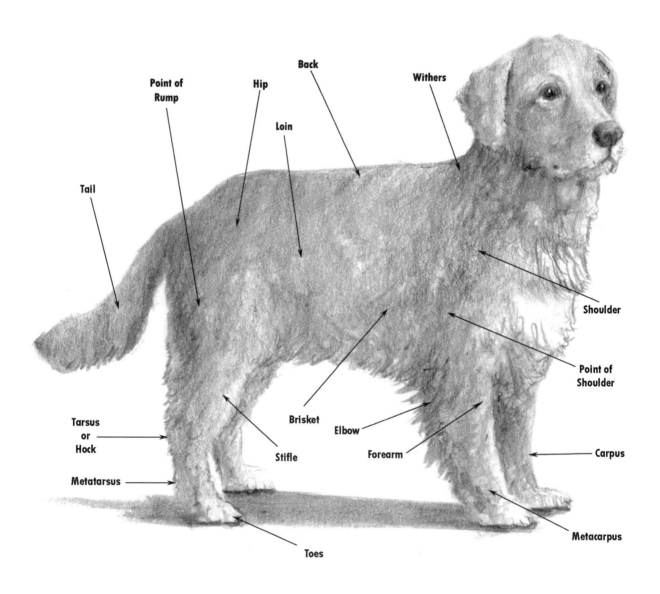

Back

Point of
Rump

Hip

Loin

Withers

Tail

Shoulder

Point of
Shoulder

Tarsus
or
Hock

Brisket

Elbow

Forearm

Carpus

Stifle

Metatarsus

Metacarpus

Toes

HEAD ANATOMY

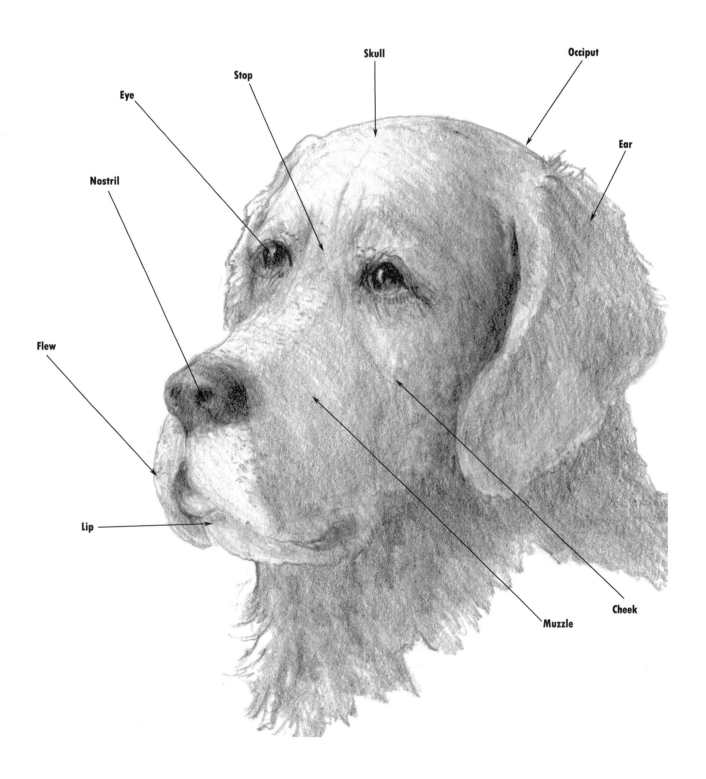

Skull

Occiput

Stop

Eye

Ear

Nostril

Flew

Lip

Cheek

Muzzle

Styling by Mixing and Matching

This section illustrates some of the different styles that I typically put my mutt clients into. I've organized it by body parts, including head, ears, body, legs, feet, and tails. This will allow you to quickly find specific styles and to compare them side by side, letting you see what styles you might want to use on the various parts of your mutts.

I've also included instructions on how to create each one of these styles and a list of the equipment to use.

Another reason for arranging the material in this fashion is to encourage you to mix and match various classic pure-breed styles to come up with your own unique styling combinations that would look just right on a mutt, but perhaps not on a purebred dog. Remember, now is your time to be creative. Nothing is wrong to attempt so "Go for it!" Keep in mind that because there are no standards for grooming a mutt, no style you might select could be wrong. Go ahead and mix and match if you think that is the look you want to achieve.

So, let's get started and take a close up look at some classic head stylings that work well on the mutt.

Head Styles

Shih Tzu

Equipment:
- Straight Scissor
- Comb
- Latex Band

1. Trim the inside corners of the eyes with scissors.

2. To form the topknot, part the hair evenly from the outside eye corners to the ears, over the top of each ear and across the back of the skull using the farthest point of the eartops as the line to follow.

3. Center the top knot and wrap a latex band around it.

4. Attach a small bow to the front of the top knot.

Lhasa Apso

Equipment:

- Straight Scissor
- Comb

1. Trim the inside corners of the eyes.

2. Part the hair evenly using the last tooth of the comb.

34

West Highland White Terrier

Equipment:

- Slicker brush
- Comb
- Clipper
- #10 blade
- Thinning shears
- Curved scissor
- Straight scissor

1. Clip the upper one-third of the ears with a #10 blade on both sides. Trim the clipped portion of the ear to the leather with straight scissors.

2. Trim the inside eye corners with straight scissors.

3. With curved scissors, taper down the remaining portion of the ear widening as you go to blend it into the circle of the head.

4. The shaved ear tips should peek out over the top of the circle. End the circle using curved scissors at the base of the skull with it continuing to a full circle.

5. With thinning shears, go over the edges to give it a natural appearance.

Cairn Terrier

Equipment:

- Slicker brush
- Comb
- Clipper
- #10 blade
- Thinning shears
- Curved scissor
- Straight scissor

1. Use a #10 blade to clip the ear from the base to the tip on both sides and scissor the edges to the leather.

2. Round the head with straight or curved scissors leaving the ear tips showing above the circle.

3. When you have the desired shape, go over the edges of the head with thinning shears to give it a more natural appearance, being careful not to nick the ears.

Scottish Terrier

Equipment:

- Slicker brush
- Comb
- Straight scissor
- Clipper
- #7F blade
- #10 blade

1. Use a #10 or a #7F blade on top of the head, forming a "V" for the eyebrows.

2. Continue with the same blade and clip between the ears and outside the eye corners.

3. Clean under the eyes with a #10 blade and along the sides of the face and down the front of the neck to the Adam's apple forming a "U" or "neck-lace."

4. Scissor between the brows and sharply triangulate them.

5. Comb the beard length forward.

Miniature Schnauzer

Equipment:

- Slicker brush
- Comb
- Straight scissor
- Clipper
- #7F blade
- #10 blade

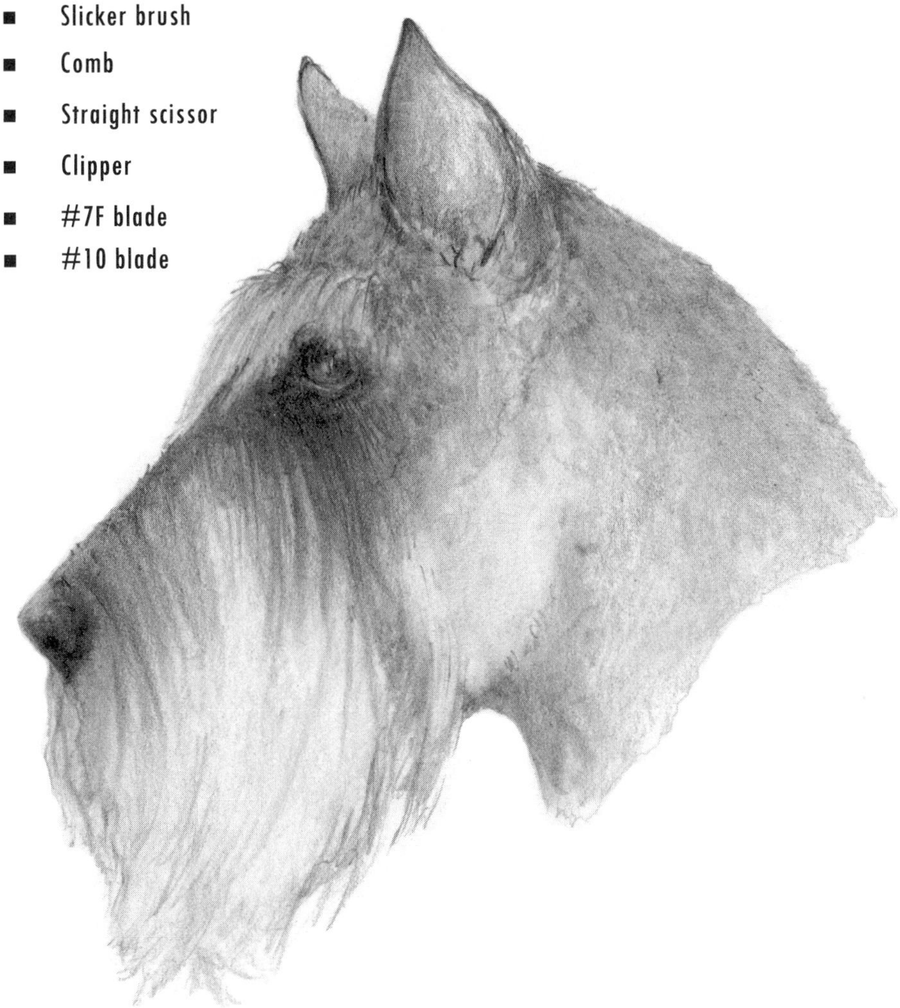

1. Use a #10 or #7F blade on top of the head, forming a "V" for the eyebrows.

2. Continue with the same blade and clip between the ears and the outside eye corners. Clean under the eyes with a #10 blade, along the sides of the face and down the front of the neck to the Adam's apple forming a "U" or "necklace."

3. Scissor between the brow and then triangulate them.

4. Comb the beard forward.

Brussels Griffon

Equipment:

- Slicker brush
- Comb
- Clipper
- #4F blade
- Thinning shears
- Straight scissor

1. Use a #4F blade on top of the head and straight down the sides of the face between the outside eye corners and underneath the ears. Do not go under the face. Leave beneath the clipped area as part of the beard.

2. Scissor the beard to look rounded but the length remains full. Fluff the beard out but not forward.

3. Scissor the ear edges to the leather with straight scissors.

Border Terrier

Equipment:

- Comb
- Clipper
- #40 blade to use with the
- 3/8" (#2) snap on comb
- Thinning shears
- Straight scissor

1. Use a #3/8" (#2) snap on comb on top of the head leaving enough for a small visor.

2. Curve the beard from the front to the outside eye corners and shape the visor short.

3. Trim the outside edges of the ears to the leather with thinning shears.

Kerry Blue Terrier

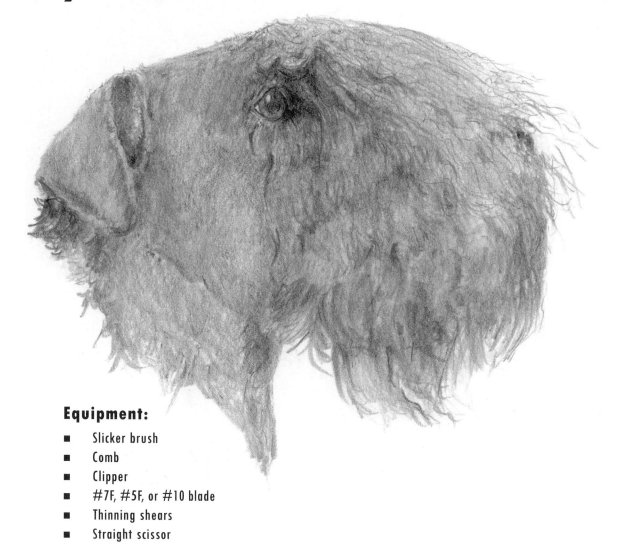

Equipment:

- Slicker brush
- Comb
- Clipper
- #7F, #5F, or #10 blade
- Thinning shears
- Straight scissor

1. Use a #10, #7F, or #5F blade on top of the head clip a "V" above the brows. Do not scissor between them. This hair will flow foward down the nose forming the fall.

2. Comb the eyebrows forward, point the thinning shears toward the nose, being careful to keep the point away from the eyes, and trim the brows just over the eyes to make the eyes visible.

3. With a #10 blade, clip from underneath the ears to the inside eye corners cleaning under the eye and down the throat to the Adam's apple forming a "U" or "necklace."

4. Using a #10, #7F or #5F blade on top of the ears and a #10 blade inside the ear and trim them to the leather.

Soft Coated Wheaten Terrier

Equipment:

- Slicker brush
- Comb
- Clipper
- #5F blade
- #40 blade to use with the
- #3/8" (#2) snap on comb
- Thinning shears
- Straight scissor

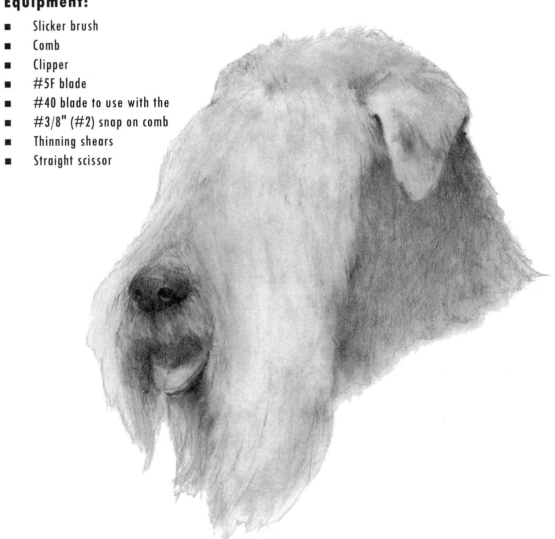

1. Use a #3/8" (#2) snap on comb over approximately two-thirds of the back skull, starting in front of the ear and continuing to the occiput. Blend the hair on the back of the skull into the hair on the neck with thinning shears.

2. Continue down the sides of the face behind the outer eye corner and beneath the ear with the #3/8" (#2) snap on comb. Let the rest fall forward down the nose.

3. Use a #5F blade on top of the ear and scissor the edge of the leather to neaten.

Bichon Frise

Equipment:
- Slicker brush
- Comb
- Curved scissor
- Straight scissor

1. With straight or curved scissors, scissor above the eyes straight across the stop.

2. Using curved or straight scissors, scissor just above and below the eyes to accent them.

3. Round the top of the head over the skull from ear to ear. Shorten the bottoms of the ears almost to the leather and while rounding the sides of the face, incorporate the ears into the circle by beveling their bottoms.

4. Continue the circle by rounding the beard in proportion to the rest of the head.

Poodle

Equipment:

- Slicker brush
- Comb
- Clipper
- #10 blade
- Curved scissor

1. Use a #10 blade to clean the face using the outside eye corners as the pattern. Clip straight back to underneath the ears. Shave the muzzle, forming an inverted "V" at the stop. Clip down the throat to the Adam's apple to form a "necklace."

2. Brush the topknot forward from the base of the skull and scissor a circle using the stop, the top of the ears and the base of the skull as your pattern. Repeat the circle after brushing it back and then side to side. Fluff up and even it.

3. Use a #10 blade to clip the top third of the ear. Trim the edges of the shaved area with straight scissors. **Note:** The ears can also be left full and natural.

44

Dandie Dinmont Terrier

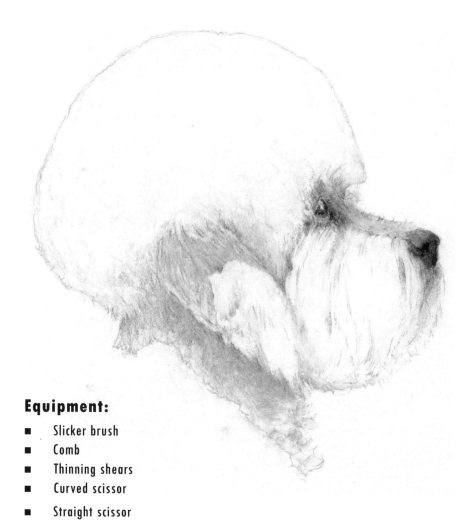

Equipment:

- Slicker brush
- Comb
- Thinning shears
- Curved scissor
- Straight scissor

1. Clean out around the eyes, stop and top of the nose to make the eyes appear as large as possible.

2. Brush the topknot forward from the base of the skull and even it off across the front, softly framing the eyes by extending the bangs over the eyes slightly.

3. Fluff it up and continue scissoring around the head slightly extending over the ears and skull. Keep scissoring until you get the appearance of a large chrysanthemum that is rounded, high and fluffy.

4. Thin the cheeks out and tassel the ears.

Bedlington Terrier

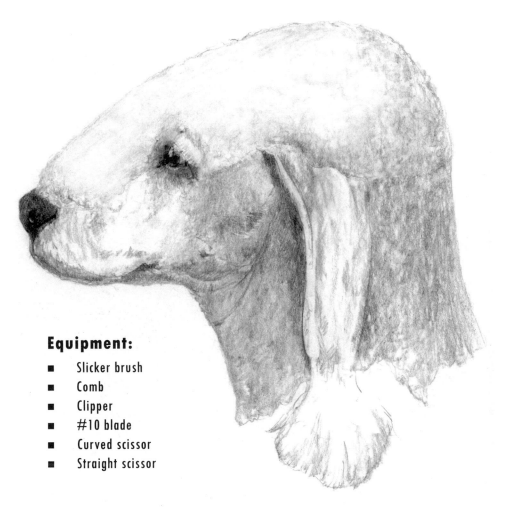

Equipment:

- Slicker brush
- Comb
- Clipper
- #10 blade
- Curved scissor
- Straight scissor

1. Use a #10 blade from the outside ear corner to the outside corner of the eyes. Continue from the corner of the eyes to behind the corners of the mouth.

2. Clip the entire underjaw continuing down the neck to form a deep "V" just below the Adam's apple.

3. Scissor the head flat on the sides blending up into a full topknot, leaving the hair close at the sides and full at the top. Scissor the topknot evenly from the base of the neck to the tip of the nose giving it a lamb's appearance.

4. Scissor the muzzle around in proportion to the head. The front view of the head is to appear long and straight and it arches across the top between the ears. Taper the muzzle slightly and tassel the ears.

American Cocker Spaniel

Equipment:

- Slicker brush
- Comb
- Clipper
- #10 blade
- #7 blade or
- #5F blade
- Thinning shears
- Straight scissor

1. Use a #10, #7F, or #5F blade on the back two-thirds of the head.

2. Use a #10 blade all around the muzzle, the outside corner of the eye to underneath the ears and down the throat to the Adam's apple forming a "U" or "necklace."

3. For the crown, blend the front one-third top of the head with thinning shears into the back two-thirds of the head. This builds the forehead up and gives it a square appearance.

    OR

    Use a #10, #7F, or #5F blade on the entire skull. Use a #10 blade outside the corners of the eyes to underneath the ears and down the throat to the Adam's apple forming a "U" or "necklace."

Petit Basset Griffon Vendeen

Equipment:

- Comb
- Thinning shears
- Stripping knife (optional)

1. The head as well as the body is to appear tousled and scruffy. Using thinning shears, scissor anything detracting from the good general outline of the head and ears. You may hand strip if you prefer, using the stripping knife.

2. Slightly triangulate the eyebrows with thinning shears and leave the beard full.

3. Scissor the inside eye corners.

48

Papillon

Equipment:

- Comb

1. Comb the head and the ear feathers. Leave the ears long and flowing for an elegant butterfly look.

Shih Tzu *(Pet Puppy Cut)*

Equipment:

- Slicker brush
- Clipper
- #40 blade to use with the
- #3/8", #½" or #5/8" snap on comb
- Thinning shears
- Curved scissor
- Straight scissor

1. Trim the inside eye corners with straight scissors.

2. Comb the hair from the occiput forward and scissor short bangs to frame the face using curved scissors.

3. Continue with the curved scissors down each side and round the bottom of the beard into the circle.

4. Shorten the ears and bevel the bottoms to incorporate them into the circle also with the curved scissors.

5. If the top of the head still appears too long, fluff it up and with curved scissors or a snap on comb shorten it. Use the comb size that is in proportion to the rest of the coat and body. Blend where it is needed with thinning shears, such as the tops and bottoms of the ears, and the sides of the face.

Ear Styles

Ears need to be treated as a separate subject since there can be a variation to the ways the ears are treated in the previous head styling section. You may see something on an ear page you would like to incorporate somewhere else, so always keep your mind and your eyes open.

Bichon Frise Ears

Equipment:
- Slicker brush
- Comb
- Curved scissor

With a curved scissor, shorten the bottom of the ear feathers almost to the leather. While rounding the sides of the face, incorporate the ears into the circle by beveling their bottoms.

Shih Tzu Ears (Pet Puppy Cut)

Equipment:
- Slicker brush
- Comb
- Curved scissor

With a curved scissor, shorten the ear almost to the leather and fluff the ear feathering out. Continue the circle from the top of the head down and around the ear, and bevel the bottoms of the ears into the circle.

Maltese Ears with Pigtails

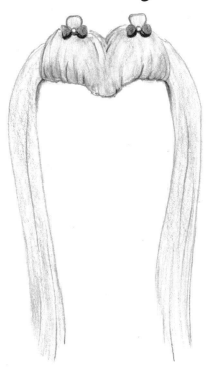

Equipment:

- Comb
- Latex bands

Allow the ear length to continue to grow. Comb the hair straight back from the brow. Part it evenly from the outside eye corners to the ears, over the top of each ear, across the back of the skull using the ear tops as the line to follow, and down the center with a comb. Twist this section. Then fold down creating a nub and wrap a rubber band around it. Repeat this process on the other side.

Yorkshire Terrier Ears with a Topknot

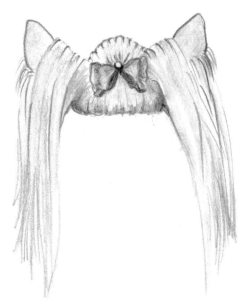

Equipment:

- Comb
- Clipper
- #10 blade
- Latex band

Clip the upper ½ of the ears with a #10 blade on both sides. Trim the clipped portion of the ear to the leather with straight scissors. Part evenly from outside the eye corners to the ears over the top of each ear and across the back of the skull using the eartops as the line to follow. Center the topknot and wrap a rubber band around it.

Cairn Terrier

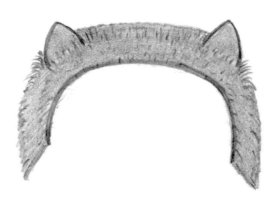

Equipment:

- Comb
- Clipper
- #10 blade
- Straight scissor

Clip the entire ear on both sides with a #10 blade. Trim the edges of the ear to the leather with straight scissors. The shaved ears should peek out over the top of the circle of the head.

West Highland White Terrier ("Westie")

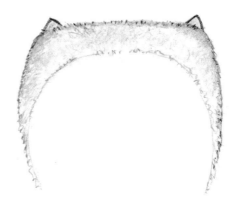

Equipment:

- Comb
- Clipper
- #10 blade
- Curved scissor
- Straight scissor

Clip the upper one-third of the ears with a #10 blade on both sides. Trim the clipped portion of the ear to the leather with straight scissors. With curved scissors, taper down the remaining portion of the ear widening as you go to blend it into the circle of the head. The shaved ear tips should peek out over the top of the circle.

Kerry Blue Terrier Ears

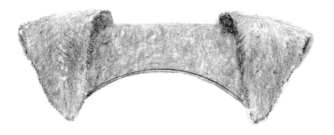

Equipment:
- Clipper
- #10 blade
- #7F or #5F blade
- Straight scissor

Use a #7F or #5F blade on the top of the ear leather and a #10 blade to clip the inside of the ear leather. Scissor the ears to the leather with a straight scissor.

Soft Coated Wheaten Terrier Ears

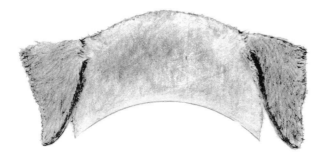

Equipment:
- Clipper
- #10 blade
- #7F or #5F blade
- Straight scissor

Use a #10, #7F, or a #5F blade to clip the top of the ear leather and use a #10 blade to clip the inside ear leather. Scissor the ears to the leather with a straight scissor.

American Cocker Spaniel Ears

Equipment:

- Slicker brush
- Comb
- Clipper
- #10, #15, #30 blade
- Straight scissor

Use a #10, #15 or #30 blade to clip the top one-third of the ear. Start at the top where the ear connects to the head for measurement. It ends at the bottom of the feathering. Trim the edges of the shaved areas with straight scissors.

Golden Retriever Ears

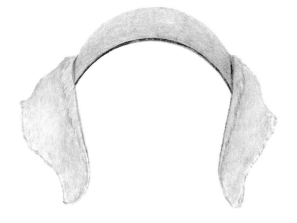

Equipment:

- Comb
- Thinning Shears

Comb the long ear feathers toward the back of the ear and shorten them using thinning shears along the leather's edges. Repeat this process combing the feathers to the front of the ear. Comb the shortened feathers straight down and neaten with thinning shears until the ear looks neat but natural.

Papillon Ears

Equipment:
- Comb

The ears stand up and the hair is left long and flowing for an elegant butterfly look.

Skye Terrier Ears

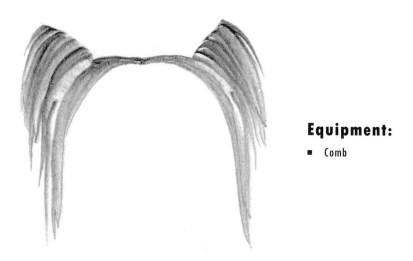

Equipment:
- Comb

These ears also stand up and the hair is long and flowing for an elegant look.

Scottish Terrier Ears

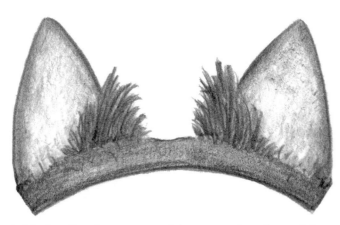

Equipment:
- Comb
- Clipper
- #10 blade
- Thinning Shears
- Straight scissor

Using a #10 blade clip the outer and inner ear leaving a fringe on the inside bottom half edge of the ear and out of the ear canal, forming a "tuft." To set the pattern for the ear tuft length, bend the ear leather in half backwards and smooth the tuft and fringe up to the fold. Cut across using a straight scissor then trim the rest of the ear to the leather.

Dandie Dinmont Terrier Ears

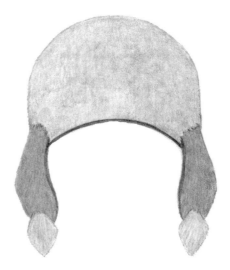

Equipment:
- Comb
- Clipper
- #10 blade
- Straight scissor

Lift the overflowing topknot to start clipping at the top of the ear, where the ear connects to the leather, and using a #10 blade, clip down the leather. Leave the feathers at the bottom of the leather in an inverted "V." Shape the bottom of the tassel to a point with thinning shears forming it into a diamond shape. Trim the clipped ear edges with a straight scissor to neaten.

Body Styles

Golden Retriever Body

Equipment:

- Slicker brush
- Comb
- V Rake
- Shedding blade or
- Stripping knife
- Thinning shears

1. Brush over the back and the sides using the slicker brush, shedding blade and/or stripping knife. Neaten with thinning shears remembering to leave a natural look.

60

Bichon Frise Body

Equipment:

- Slicker Brush
- Comb
- Clipper
- #10 blade
- Curved scissor
- Straight scissor

1. Using long straight scissors trim the coat to approximately 2" all over starting at the base of the tail pointing toward the neck and continuing down the sides.

2. Accent the brisket by working up to the loin tuck up.

Shih Tzu Body
(Pet Puppy Cut)

Equipment:

- Comb
- Clipper
- #10 blade
- #40 blade to use with the
- #3/8" (#2), #½", #5/8",
- #¾" or #1" Snap on Comb
- Curved scissor
- Straight scissor

1. Depending on how long you wish to leave the coat length use a #5F or #4F blade, or a #3/8" (#2), #½", #5/8", #¾" or #1" snap on comb from the base of the skull to the base of the tail on both the body, and the legs, and all around the body.

2. Fluff up and even with a straight scissor. If a softer look is desired use the curved scissor. It leaves a little softer look because it only takes a small amount of hair.

62

Scottish Terrier Body

Equipment:

- Slicker brush
- Comb
- Clipper
- #7 blade
- #10 blade
- Thinning shears

1. Use a #7F blade from the back of the skull to the base of the tail.

2. Bring the clipper straight down the sides from the elbow to just below the rectum all around the body. Do not go under the body.

3. Blend where it's needed with thinning shears and leave the skirt length.

Miniature Schnauzer Body

Equipment:

- Slicker brush
- Comb
- Clipper
- #5F blade
- #7 or #10 blade
- Thinning shears

1. Use a #10, #7F or #5F blade from the base of the skull to the base of the tail. Make another stroke on each side of the first to widen this area. The rest of the clipped area of the body will be done with the clipper blade pointing straight down to the table. This blends the clipped area of the body into the skirt.

2. Continue straight down the sides to leave a skirt. Do not go under the body.

3. Blend the clipped sides into the skirt with thinning shears where it's needed and trim the bottom of the skirt angling from the brisket up to the loin tuck up.

Soft Coated Wheaten Terrier Body

Equipment:

- Slicker brush
- Comb
- Clipper
- #10 blade
- #40 blade to use with the
- 5/8" snap on comb
- Thinning shears

1. Use a #5/8" snap on comb from the base of the skull to the base of the tail. Clip straight down the sides. Do not go under the body. This blends the shorter body hair into the longer skirt hair and the longer leg hair.

2. Scissor the skirt short with thinning shears angling from the brisket up to the tuck up of the loin.

Lowchen Body

Equipment:

- Slicker brush
- Comb
- Clipper
- #15 blade
- #10 or #7F blade

1. Use a #15, #10 or #7F blade from the last rib to and including the hindquarters leaving the front full and natural.

Dandie Dinmont Terrier Body

1. Use #5F blade and beginning two fingers width down from the base of the skull clip to the base of the tail. Make another stroke on each side of the first to widen this area. The rest of the clipped area of the body will be done with the clipper blade pointing straight down to the table. This blends the clipped area of the body into the skirt.

2. Continue clipping straight down the sides to leave a skirt. Do not go under the body. With thinning shears, make the skirt 1½–2" long from the brisket to the loin tuck up. Blend the clipped sides into the skirt with the thinning shears.

Equipment:

- Comb
- Clipper
- #10 blade
- #5F blade
- Thinning shears

Petit Basset Griffon Vendeen Body

Equipment:

- Clipper
- #10 blade
- Comb
- Thinning shears
- Stripping knife (to card)

1. A PeeBee-GeeVee's coat is usually between 1–2" long, rough and wiry. With your fingers, pluck or use thinning shears to even out any exceptionally long guard hairs that may detract from the appearance.

West Highland White Terrier Body

Equipment:

- Comb
- Clipper
- #10 blade
- #7F, #5F, or #4F blade
- #40 blade to use with the
- #3/8 (#2) snap on comb
- Thinning shears

1. Use a #7F, #5F or #4F blade or a #3/8" (#2) snap on comb from the back of the skull to the base of the tail make another stroke on each side of the first to widen this area. The rest of the clipped area of the body will be done with the clipper blade pointing straight down to the table. This blends the shaved area of the body into the skirt.

2. Continue straight down the sides to leave a skirt. Do not go under the body.

3. Blend the clipped sides into the skirt with thinning shears where it is need and neaten the bottom of the skirt.

Cairn Terrier Body

Equipment:

- Comb
- Clipper
- #10 blade
- #7F, #5F, or #4F blade
- #40 blade to use with the
- #3/8 (#2) snap on comb
- Thinning shears

1. Use thinning shears to thin out the body. Make 2–3 cuts, starting close to the skin and working out, cutting a small to medium section at a time. Make the coat length shorter on the back getting gradually longer for the skirt. Thin out until you achieve the desired look.

OR

1. Use a #7F, #5F or #4F blade or a #3/8" (#2) snap on comb from the base of the skull to the base of the tail. Make another stroke on each side of the first to widen this area. The rest of the clipped area of the body will be done with the clipper blade pointing straight down to the table. This blends the clipped area of the body into the skirt.

2. Continue straight down the sides to leave a skirt. Do not go under the body.

3. Blend the clipped sides into the skirt with thinning shears where it is needed and neaten the bottom of the skirt.

Note: Remember, this dog is to look natural.

American Cocker Spaniel Body

Equipment:

- Slicker brush
- Comb
- Clipper
- #7F or #10 blade
- Thinning shears

1. Using a #10 or #7F blade clip from the base of the skull to the base of the tail. Make another stroke on each side of the first to widen this area. The rest of the clipped area of the body will be done with the clipper blade pointing straight down to the table. This blends the clipped area of the body into the skirt.

2. Continue straight down the sides to leave a skirt. Do not go under the body.

3. Blend the clipped sides into the skirt with thinning shears where it is needed and neaten the bottom edge of the skirt.

Leg & Feet Styles

Another quick change for the "Designer Dog" is to change the leg style until you find the one that works best for him. Leg styles can hide a bunch of imperfections. Just use your imagination!

Remember, the dog's nails need to be cut before the bath, not after, in case you cut the quick and the dog bleeds onto its coat. When you groom in this sequence, you will never have to rebathe the dog.

Piped with Angulated Back Legs

Equipment:

- ◼ Slicker brush
- ◼ Comb
- ◼ Curved scissor
- ◼ Straight scissor
- ◼ Nail trimmer

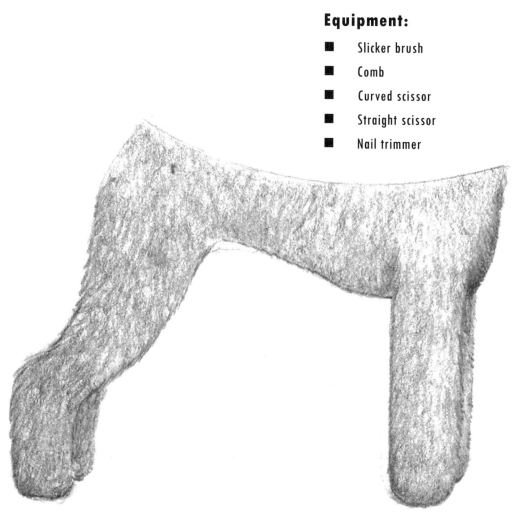

1. Pick up each foot and while looking at the bottom, make the first cut straight across the front of the foot with curved scissors. This first cut avoids a pointed look.

2. Continue by scissoring around the outer edges of the pads. On the front legs use straight scissors and point straight from the shoulder down to the table and around to create a cylindrical shape.

3. Angulate the back leg with a curved scissor to the shape of the leg turning the curve of the shear to coincide with the leg's curve. Bevel around each foot.

Piped Legs

Equipment:

- Slicker brush
- Comb
- Curved scissor
- Straight scissor
- Nail trimmer

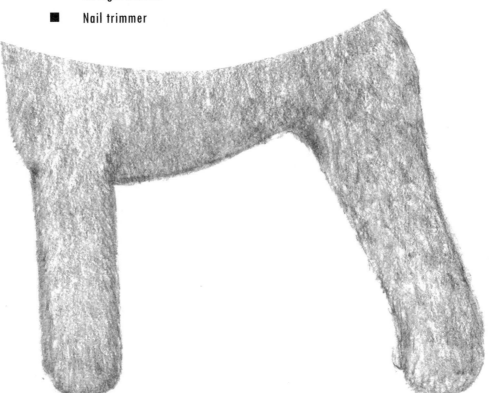

1. Pick up each foot and while looking at the bottom, make the first cut straight across the front of the foot with curved scissor. This first cut avoids a pointed look. Continue by scissoring around the outer edges of the pads.

2. On the front legs use straight scissors pointing straight from the shoulder down to the table and around to create a cylindrical shape. Repeat the same process only from the hip on the back legs.

3. Bevel around each foot.

Pantaloons With Poodle Feet

Equipment:

- Slicker Brush
- Comb
- Clipper
- #30 blade
- #7F, #5F or #4F blade
- Curved Scissor
- Straight scissor
- Nail trimmer

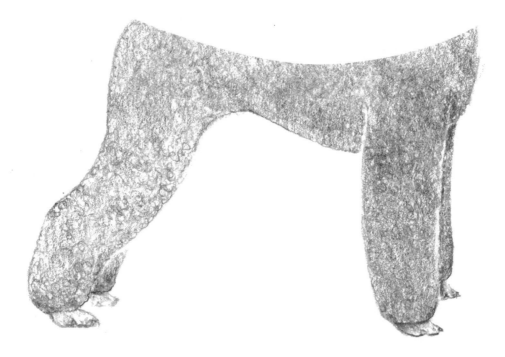

1. For Poodle feet use a #30 blade, going against the grain, clip up the back of the front feet to the ankle pad. Clip up both sides of the feet to the same height of ankle pad. Clip between the large pad and the small pads on the bottom of the feet. Do the same with the top of the feet.

2. With your index finger between the large and smaller pads on the bottom of the foot and your thumb on the top spread each set

Pantaloons With Poodle Feet (Cont'd.)

of toes and scoop the hair neatly out from between them with the #30 blade. Repeat for each foot, front and back.

3. Proportion is what sets the pantaloon pattern size. Pipe the front leg cylinders to the desired length using straight scissors and curved scissors to bevel the bottom cuff.

4. Scissor in the top of the front pantaloon patterns using the front and back of the leg length, approximately 1" in from the elbow, and arching over the shoulder to the desired proportionate height.

5. Softly angulate the back legs with both curved and straight scissors to match the length of the front legs. Bevel the bottom cuffs with curved scissors. Scissor in the top of the back pantaloon patterns, using the front and back of the leg length, approximately 1" in from the flank, and arching over the hip, matching the height of the front pantaloons.

6. Use a #7F, #5F or #4F blade from the base of the skull to the base of the tail. Continue down the sides of the body going with the grain and cut out the pattern already set with your scissors.

7. Neaten the curve of the pantaloon tops with curved scissors and with straight scissors match the hair length on the top of the pantaloon to the hair length of the leg.

Note: The fuller you pipe the legs the larger the pantaloon pattern will be.

76

Bracelets with Poodle Feet

Equipment:

- Slicker Brush
- Comb
- Clipper
- #30 blade
- #10 blade
- Curved scissor
- Nail trimmer

1.   For Poodle feet, use a #30 blade, going against the grain, clip up the back of the front feet to the ankle pad. Clip up both sides of the feet to the same height of the ankle pad. Do the same with the top of the feet.

2.   With your index finger between the large and smaller pads on the bottom of the foot and your thumb on the top spread each set of toes and scoop the hair neatly out from between them with the #30 blade. Repeat for each foot, front and back.

3.   Clip all around the back leg with a #10 blade to the hock joint.

4.   Brush all of the bracelet hair up from the clipped foot and scissor around the top with the convex side of the curved scissor pointing up—high side of the curves pointing up—toward the dog's brisket.

Bracelets with Poodle Feet (Cont'd.)

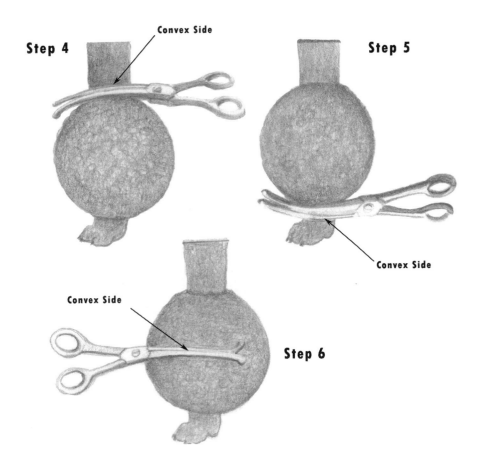

5. Repeat this process by brushing the bracelet down and with the convex side of the curved scissor pointing down—high side of the curves pointing down—toward the table.

6. Using the comb, fluff the bracelet bottom up toward the center of the pompon, and the top down toward the center of the pompon and scissor around the center of the pompon with the high point of the curved scissors—high side of the curves—pointing away from the circle.

7. Fluff the bracelet out and neaten it. Repeat on the other back leg.

8. Clip the front legs down to the height of the bracelets on the back legs and repeat the bracelet scissoring instructions on each of the front legs.

Schnauzer Legs

Equipment:

- Comb
- Clipper
- #5, #7F, or #10 Blade
- Slicker Brush
- Straight scissor
- Curved scissor
- Nail trimmer

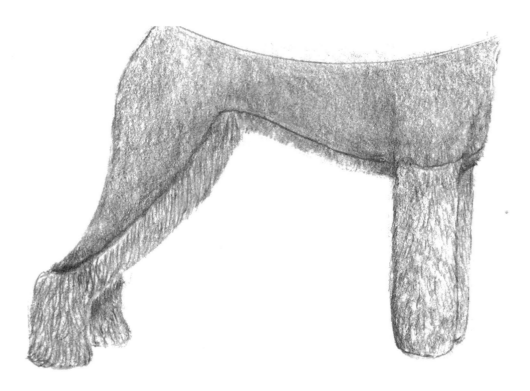

1. Use a #10, #7F, or #5 blade down the back half of the rear legs to a point just above the hock.

2. Shape the fringe with the curved scissor to curve with the stifle (knee) and with the straight scissors pipe from the hock down.

3. Pipe the front legs with straight scissor. Round and bevel the feet with curved scissors.

Bell Bottom Legs

Equipment:

- Comb
- Slicker Brush
- Curved scissor
- Straight scissor
- Nail trimmer

1. Trim the feet with curved scissors into a large circle.

2. Allow the silky hair on the legs to flow down into the large foot forming bell bottoms.

West Highland White Terrier Legs

Equipment:

- ■ Slicker brush
- ■ Comb
- ■ Thinning shears
- ■ Curved scissor
- ■ Nail clipper

1. Round the feet with curved scissors and let the legs and skirt grow and flow.

2. Blend the back into the legs and skirt with thinning shears and neaten as needed.

Cairn Terrier Legs

Equipment:

- Slicker brush
- Comb
- Thinning shears
- Curved scissor
- Nail clipper

1. Round the feet with curved scissors.

2. With thinning shears, thin out the coat where it is needed by making 2–3 cuts, starting close to the skin and working out. Cut a small to medium section at a time.

3. Neaten the legs with thinning shears.

Note: This dog is to look natural.

Tail Styles

It seems appropriate to have this section at the tail-end of the Mix and Match Styling section. Tails are a good focal point, so use your imagination and creativity to make your mutt look extra special.

Carrot Tail

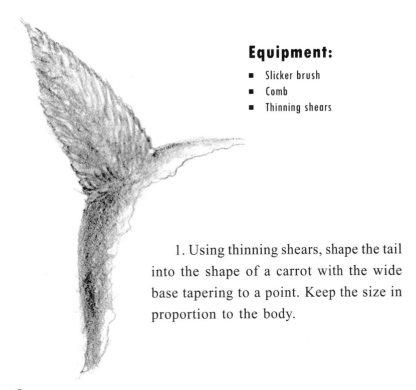

Equipment:

- Slicker brush
- Comb
- Thinning shears

1. Using thinning shears, shape the tail into the shape of a carrot with the wide base tapering to a point. Keep the size in proportion to the body.

Pompon Tail

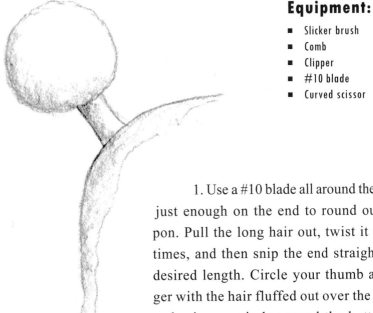

Equipment:

- Slicker brush
- Comb
- Clipper
- #10 blade
- Curved scissor

1. Use a #10 blade all around the tail leaving just enough on the end to round out the pompon. Pull the long hair out, twist it a couple of times, and then snip the end straight off to the desired length. Circle your thumb and forefinger with the hair fluffed out over the top of them and scissor a circle around the bottom of what is resting on your hand. Repeat this process two more times after pulling your hand up a little more each time. Let it go, fluff it out and reshape it.

Plumed Tail

Equipment:

- Slicker brush
- Comb
- Thinning shears

1. Hold the tail straight out from the body and shorten and neaten the bottom of the feathers to the desired length with thinning shears.

Sickle Tail

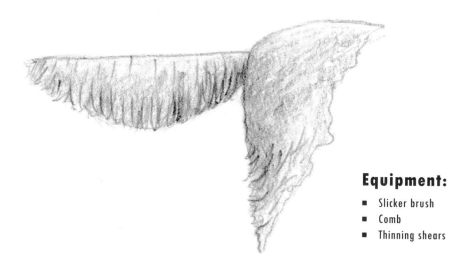

Equipment:

- Slicker brush
- Comb
- Thinning shears

1. Scissor the tail with thinning shears tapering it at the tip and the base of tail and lengthening it in the center.

Fox Tail

Equipment:

- Slicker brush
- Comb
- Thinning shears

1. Shape the tail with thinning shears pointing at the tip and widening out at the base in proportion to the body length.

Rat Tail

Equipment:

- Slicker brush
- Comb
- Clipper
- #10 blade
- Curved scissor

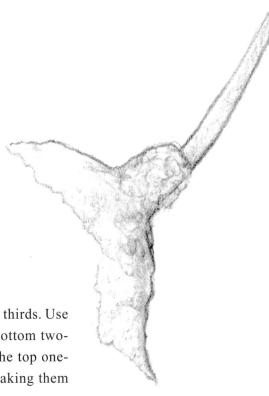

1. Divide the tail into thirds. Use a #10 blade to clip the bottom two-thirds to the tip. Blend the top one-third into the body by making them the same length.

Lion Tail

Equipment:

- Comb
- Clipper
- #10 blade

1. Use a #10 blade and clip all around the tail half-way to the tip leaving a plume (natural) on the end.

Chapter Three

Underplaying Physical Imperfections with Grooming Corrections

Groomers will accept new clients for grooming even if they are not purebred dogs. Therefore, we have to know how to groom a funny-shaped dog in a way that makes it look its best. As discussed in the previous chapter, one way to do that is to pick out the dominant breed in the mutt and style accordingly. Another very important way to make a mutt look its best is to underemphasize anatomical imperfections with grooming corrections.

As a lecturer at seminars, I'm often barraged with questions from the groomers in the audience on how to fix or underplay a mutt's physical imperfections. For instance:

"What can be done for the dog with slew feet?

"I have a little Cockapoo without a definite stop. What's the best way to deal with this problem?"

"What can I do for a Shih Tzu mix with "windmill ears?"

"What can be done when a mutt's head is smaller than its body?"

In order to be able to meet these challenges with success, start out by knowing good general canine anatomy and body structure. This will give you a basic foundation from which to identify those conditions that need underplaying. Again know your breeds! Being proficient in these two areas, along with using your common sense and imagination will make you an outstanding stylist that earns the reputation for being a "Mutt Magician." This reputation will be further enhanced when your clients tell you how thrilled they are to see their precious mutt companion transformed into a beauty.

I created this chapter because as a dog groomer, in the trenches daily, I know that time is money. I felt that if I listed common problems we deal with when we style mutts and some quick solutions, it would make your life easier.

I hope these few suggestions give you some ideas. Use your imagination because nothing you do is wrong. Remember to have fun and keep in mind that here are no ugly mutts, just challenges waiting for a stylist.

The following chapter is broken into three sections. Section one lists questions and solutions for the face, head and ears. Section two lists questions and solutions pertaining to imperfections in the dog's body and tail. Section three addresses the legs and feet. Common questions for each problem area will be listed and definitions for any relevant terms will be given, along with suggested solutions. Where appropriate, drawings will demonstrate some of the terms and concepts described in this section. I am sure you will find this question and answer format helpful.

Well, let's get the mutt magic started, we have a lot to cover!

Correcting Imperfections
of the
Face, Head & Ears

Q **What can be done to help cover up an overshot or an undershot jaw?**

A If at all possible, use facial hair to cover either one of these conditions. With a little "mutt magic," give the dog a modified Bichon head, or if the hair texture permits it, style a Schnauzer beard. A donut moustache would certainly be dapper too. Any face having a beard and fall will help to cover up projecting teeth and will also draw attention away from them.

def.

Undershot jaw is the front teeth of the lower jaw protruding over the upper jaw's front teeth when the mouth is in a closed position.

Overshot jaw is the opposite. It's the space between the dog's front upper and lower teeth created by the upper front teeth protruding beyond the lower.

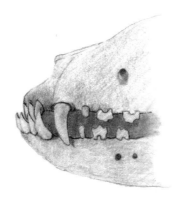

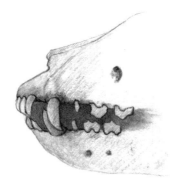

Donut Moustache is a small round moustache that continues to circle under the chin. It should be kept close to the nose and away from the corners of the mouth.

Fall is the hair from above the dog's eyebrows which hangs over the eyes and face. Breeds that have falls include: Airedales, Kerry Blue Terriers and Soft Coated Wheaten Terriers.

Q

This mutt has very little stop and absolutely no Collie in him! What can be done?

A

As with all mutt makeovers, many styling decisions depend on the dogs' coat type. If the coat type can support it, create a stop as I did for Cameo on pages 154-159. The first way was to build up a Cocker Spaniel crown. The second was to style her in a modified Bichon head to cover up her lack of a stop. My last suggestion is when everything else fails, hide it! Create a fall by mimicking a Kerry Blue Terrier or Soft Coated Wheaten Terrier face. See Reba on page 162 for instructions.

def.

Stop is the area where the muzzle meets the skull between the eyes.

Blend this technique is often used because it adds a more natural look to the dog. It is the union of two lengths of hair with thinning shears, a skip tooth clipper blade (the size already being used or one size longer cut) or a snap on comb one size longer than the one already used. Blending is important because it eliminates the "shelf" or "hula" look.

Crown is the hair on the front of the topskull from the eyebrows back approximately ¼ of the skull length. This hair is blended into the rest of the skull to give the head a more squared off appearance, for example the American Cocker Spaniel.

Q

What can be done to give the illusion of a muzzle being shorter or longer than it actually is?

A

To have a muzzle appear shorter, clip the dog's face using a #10 blade, leaving a small donut on the end of the muzzle.

To have the muzzle appear longer, using a #10 blade, clip the entire face clean.

Q **What can be done for the dog that has a bigger body and a smaller head?**

A Size the body down by giving it a very short cut with a #4F blade. Switch to a 5/8" snap on comb for the legs to make them appear fuller, avoiding a "toothpick leg" look. Blend where the #4F blade stops and the 5/8" snap on comb begins. The modified Bichon head goes well with this body style, like Cameo is sporting on page 158.

An alternative style is to give the body a Schnauzer cut. With a #10 blade continuing straight down the sides creating a very short skirt, angling from the brisket up to the loin tuck-up. With a #10 blade clip down the back half of the rear legs to a point just above the hock. Pipe the front legs and from the hock down on back legs. Shape the head into a modified Soft Coated Wheaten look. Using a 3/8" (#2) snap on comb, starting approximately halfway back on the skull, clip to the occiput and blend into the neck. Use thinning shears to thin out the sides of the face behind the outer eye corners until the hair lies neatly. Let the rest fall forward. Continue with thinning shears and angle brows short to long starting at the outside eye corner. Make sure to clear the dog's vision, but leave the fall intact. Scissor the ears to the leather's edge.

def. *Toothpick Legs* is one of the names that is not yet a technical term but needs to be. The dog's legs are too long and thin in proportion to the body size. They look like toothpicks were set under a large body to hold it up.

Piped legs is where the coat around the legs is scissored into a cylindrical shape resembling a pipe. Round the feet to the size you want the legs to be and use this as a pattern. Then using 8½" or 10" straight shears, scissor straight down from the shoulder or hip all around the leg. Bevel around each foot's bottom edge.

Q **In reverse, what can be done for the dog that has a smaller body and a bigger head?**

A One solution is to accent the large head by styling the dog into a Portuguese Water Dog's Lion Cut on page 130. Another option is to slim down the dog's head in a Schnauzer Clip as done with Chester on page 131. Or, try a Soft Coated Wheaten Terrier look as seen on page 129, by extensively thinning out the sides of the mutt's face to make them as thin as possible but leave the beard long.

Q **How can you cover up a knobby top of the head?**

A If the head does not have some sort of a topknot and needs to be fairly smooth, as in a Schnauzer look, use a #5F or #4F blade on top of the head. The longer the hair is the more it will cover up.

However, if you still need more, leave enough hair at the front to create a crown, as in a Cocker Spaniel look. Blend the hair into the back three-quarters of the skull which have already been clipped with the #5F or #4F blade. Blend the occiput into the neck. This will cover any other imperfections that may be present.

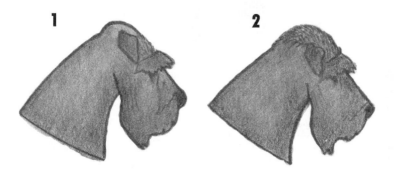

1   2

Q **What exactly are "windmill ears" and how do we work around them?**

A Eddie, on pages 120 and 123 has "windmill ears." The first rule is not to shorten the ears. Shape the ear fringe a little but don't shorten them. Blend the topknot, no matter how soft and flat it is, into the top of the ear feathering.

def. *Windmill Ears* is the name I've given to ears that normally hang down but the leather is too short so they stick out horizontally from the head.

Q **What are some short cuts for the badly matted ear?**

A If it is a hanging ear where only the bottom is matted, lift the unmatted feathers, clip the matting off of the bottom edge and let the rest of the feathering flow down over the shaved area to hide it.

If all else fails, and the ear is one big mat, clip it all off and consider styling the head with a Brussels Griffon, Border Terrier, Soft Coated Wheaten look.

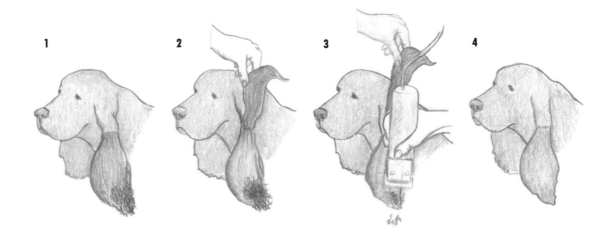

1   2   3   4

Correcting Imperfections
of the
Body & Tail

Q **How can you make a dog appear taller or shorter?**

A The easiest way to make a dog look taller is to clip or scissor the hair on its back as long as it is proportionately possible and shorten the underside as much as possible. Scissor the sides to blend the two extremes. To add to the illusion, do not forget to make the top of the dog's head as tall as possible while maintaining good proportion.

To make a dog look shorter just reverse the above answer. Scissor or clip the hair on its back as short as proportionately possible and lengthen the underside as long as possible following the body shape or work into a skirt. Blend the sides to accommodate the two extremes. Keep the top of the dog's head very short or even shorter than the back to make the height appear less imposing.

Note: Remember the 3 P's—proportion, proportion, proportion!

Legs Too Short

Legs Too Long

Legs Too Short Correction

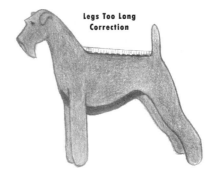

Legs Too Long Correction

Q

How can you make a dog appear longer or shorter in length?

A
Following the same premise as the above two questions, you build onto the body by making the chest, rump and back of hind legs longer. Follow the body lines.

To make the body appear shorter, reverse the above by shortening the chest, rump and back of the hind legs as short as is proportionately possible.

Q

What can be done for the dog that has a bigger body and a smaller head?

A
First size the body down by giving it a very short (#4F blade) cut, then switch to a 5/8" snap on comb for the legs to make them appear fuller, avoiding a toothpick leg look. Blend where the #4F blade stops and the 5/8" snap on comb begins. Use a modified Bichon head with this body style like Cameo is sporting on page 158.

Another alternative style would be giving the body a schnauzer cut with a #10 blade and continuing straight down the sides creating a very short skirt (angling from the brisket up to the loin tuck-up). With a #10 blade clip down the back half of the rear legs to a point just above the hock. Pipe the front legs and from the hock down on the rear legs. Shape the head into a modified Soft Coated Wheaten look. Start by using a 3/8" (#2) snap on comb starting approximately halfway back on the skull to the occiput and blend into the neck. Using a thinning shear, thin out the sides of the face behind the outer eye corner until it lies neatly. Let the rest fall forward. Continue with the thinning shears and angle the brows short to long starting at the outside eye corner to clear the vision but leaving the fall intact. Scissor the ears to the leather.

Q **In reverse, what can be done for the dog that has a smaller body and a bigger head?**

A A more extreme solution is to accent the large head by styling the dog into a Portuguese Water Dog's Lion Clip on page 130. Another option is to slim down the dog's head in a Schnauzer clip as done with Chester on page 131. Or try a Soft Coated Wheaten Terrier look as seen on page 129, by extensively thinning out the sides of the mutt's face to make them as thin as possible but leave the beard long.

Q **A Shih Tzu mix comes to my shop. He doesn't have a tail and he looks funny. How should he be styled?**

A If you like the rest of his look, then create a tail. Approximately 1" above the rectum start growing that hair from the rectum up. Let it grow until it becomes the length you want. Be sure to continue clipping and cleaning around the anus.

Q **What short cuts can be taken for a very matted dog in full coat?**

A When possible, clip out tight mats and cover with long unmatted coat to hide the bare spots. This is also a very successful technique for badly matted bottoms of hanging ears. Lift the unmatted feathers, clip matting off the bottom edge and let the rest of the feathering flow down over the shaved section to hide it.

Another suggestion for enhancing your speed is to devise a "system," or a sequence of steps involved in a groom with which you are most comfortable and will always do in that order. This prevents you from having to stop and think whether you have already clipped the nails and may even prevent you from forgetting to do it entirely! Eventually it becomes second nature and you no longer have to think about what you are doing. You'll just keep repeating it naturally and doing it more quickly as a result. I always start at the dog's left rear hip and work my way around. This saves extra steps and adds speed.

Correcting Imperfections
of the
Legs & Feet

Q **What can I do with elbows that point out?**

A Using the outermost point of the elbow for the pattern, scissor straight down to the foot, piping the leg and then scissor up to the shoulder.

Out at Elbow

Out at Elbow Correction

Q **What can I do to make the dog with front legs too close together look better?**

A When the legs are too close together, leave more hair on the outside of each leg and shorten the hair on the insides.

Narrow Front

Narrow Front Correction

Q What can I do to make the dog with legs too far apart look better?

A When the legs are too far apart, leave more hair on the inside of the legs and shorten the hair on the outside leg.

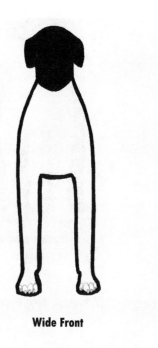

Wide Front

Wide Front Correction

Q When trimming feet like on a Golden, or a Sheltie, how can I get a clean foot and not have the nails show?

A Pick up each foot and with the bottom side pointing up, trim the pads clean and trim around the edge of the feet. Replace the foot onto the table. From the topside, pull the hair up from between the toes and with thinning shears trim the excess hair to the shape of the toes. Trim the nails last. This way the nails will not be exposed.

Note: An easy way to trim the nails of problem dogs such as caution dogs, dogs that have trouble standing on three legs, nervous dogs, and disabled dogs, is to trim them while the dog is standing, leaving the dog's foot on the table.

Q **What can be done for the dog with skinny legs and a body that looks like a sausage packed into a small casing?**

A You need to use a #10, #7F or #5F blade on the large body while scissoring down from the shoulder or hip to the foot. By shortening the body coat and building up and lengthening the leg coat you have just proportioned the dog with its own hair.

Toothpick Legs

Toothpick Legs Correction

Q **A Lhasa Apso mix comes to me that has longer front legs than back legs. What can be done?**

A Always keep the three "P's" in mind when grooming any dog. You are its beauty consultant. You want to build the hindquarters up to give the backline a level appearance. Take your 8½" straight scissors and choosing a proportionate length, scissor the coat length longer at the rump and shorter at the shoulders.

Q **What can I do if the canine has a narrow front with slew feet?**

A A way to cover both a narrow front and slew feet is to shape the legs close to the inside of each leg and build up the outside. When getting to the foot area, flare out into a bell bottom.

**Narrow Front
With Slew Feet**

**Narrow Front
With Slew Feet
Correction**

Q **This dog's elbows turn out, the pasterns are close and the feet turn out. What can be done?**

A Using the shoulder as a pattern, scissor straight down until getting to the foot area, then flare out and round into a bell bottom.

Chippendale

**Chippendale
Correction**

Q   **How can I cover up wrists that knuckle over?**

A   Starting from the front of the chest, scissor straight down until getting to the foot area, flare out and round into a bell bottom.

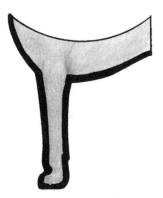

Knuckle Over

**Knuckle Over
Correction**

Q   **This dog's hind quarters are too close together. What can be done to proportion him?**

A   As with a narrow front, when the back legs are too close together leave more hair on the outside of each leg and shorten the hair on the inside legs.

**Hindquarters
Too Close**

**Hindquarters
Too Close
Correction**

Q **This dog stands like he's leaning back at the ankle. What can I do to make these legs look better?**

A Start by giving the dog poodle feet. It would be hard to cover this fault with leg furnishings (hair) since the foot extends beyond the chest. Using the chest as a pattern, scissor straight down, beveling the bottom.

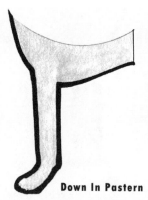

Down In Pastern

Down In Pastern
Correction

Q **I have a dog that is cow hocked. Help!**

A Try to build up the outside of the leg from the hip down as much as possible to give the leg a straight appearance. Using the inward pointing hock, scissor the inner leg from this point up and down to give a straight illusion. When scissoring down, **do not** follow the bone structure.

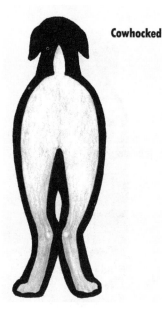

Cowhocked

Cowhocked
Correction

Q **What can I do to help the appearance of a dog with a wide rear stance?**

A Do the opposite of narrow back legs, build up the inside of the bandy legs by scissoring the hair longer. On the outside, scissor straight down from the hip making the hair as short as possible. Round the bottoms of the feet in proportion to the leg.

Bandy Legs

Bandy Legs Correction

Q **What can I do when a dog has long feet and a soft and silky coat?**

A Round the feet. Pipe the front of the leg long to the length of foot and scissor the back side of the leg short.

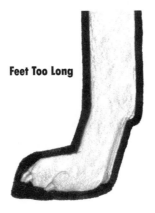

Feet Too Long

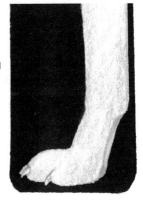

Feet Too Long Correction

Chapter Four

Making Mutt Magic—
64 Magnificent Mutt Makeovers

In this section, every one of the dogs we're working with and putting different styles on is real and each has a story that makes them special. I will be interjecting their stories here and there, because having a feel for the dogs also helps me envision their styling. It puts my heart into it, not just knowledge and skill.

All the styles are considered "modified" because we are working with one of a kind "Designer Dogs." We are striving to cover up features that are not attractive as well as accenting the dog's outstanding features.

When you see a mutt for the first time, the length of his coat can be very deceiving. This is another reason you must know your breeds. The first time you see him he might have just been shaved down or is very matted but by evaluating his background you can make suggestions to the client for future styling

For instance, let's look at Eddie on pages 122 and 123 and see why I went from his first picture being short to growing him out into a full coat.

Eddie has the body type of the Lhasa Apso but the smaller size of the Shih Tzu. He has the dense coat of the Pekingese which is soft and straight like the Shih Tzu. You can see the Shih Tzu again in Eddie's facial features and coloring.

Now look at the breeds that Eddie resembles on page 120. All three breeds (the Lhasa Apso, Pekingese and the Shih Tzu) can have floor length coats hence my conclusion that he can be styled in a full coat eventually A.K.A. "Elegant Eddie".

Are you getting the hang of it yet?

Let's go onto Jane on page 138 and 139. Jane is scruffy but her coat is short on her Introduction pages. This is exactly how she looked the first time I saw her. Now, let me explain why I visualize Jane in longer styles.

Her coat texture is soft and wavy, similar to a Cocker Spaniel's. Her size, over 15" at the shoulder and body shape coincide with the Standard Poodle's. Look at Jane's face and ears. I see both Cocker Spaniel and Standard Poodle and knowing both have their tails docked, her long tail is not deceiving.

You have to be able to see beyond no matter what kind of shape the mutt is in when you finally get to evaluate him. Know your breeds! It is an imperative key to unlocking your creativity.

Now let me explain why I set this section up the way I did.

Time is so precious, my friend, and once it's gone, we can't get it back. The point being, I assume you are a professional groomer so I won't be stating the obvious in my grooming descriptions as most grooming manuals must do. You already know that every dog gets their rectum and groin cleaned, is completely brushed out and dematted, their nails and pads clipped, their ears and eyes cleaned out as well as your final reshaping, and you don't need me reiterating these on every page.

I have also set up each of the descriptions in the same sequence and will describe and title each body section separately so you can easily scan it for specific information. This way, if you are just interested in the head and ears, just go to that section. I will also include what equipment you'll need and space for you to make notes on each page. We have enough new things to learn and accomplish without a lot of fruitless searching and repetition of steps that are second nature for you anyway. All heights listed in the descriptions are from floor to withers and lengths are from front of the chest to the back of the rump.

Bandit

I'd like you to meet Bandit, one of the cutest mutts I've ever seen. The first time I met Bandit, I fell madly in love with his size as well as his personality. He's alert, full of energy and great fun, not to mention one of a kind. In my mind I see him in so many different styles. What do you see?

Breeds that Bandit Most Resembles

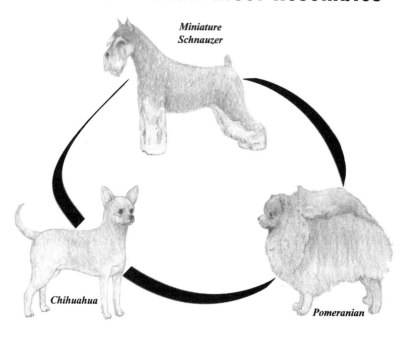

Miniature
Schnauzer

Chihuahua

Pomeranian

BANDIT'S
First Visit Evaluation Notes

Outstanding features:
alertness
bright eyes
toy size
tiny feet

Features to underplay:
large ears

Coat texture:
dense
soft
straight

Colors in coat:
black
white
gray

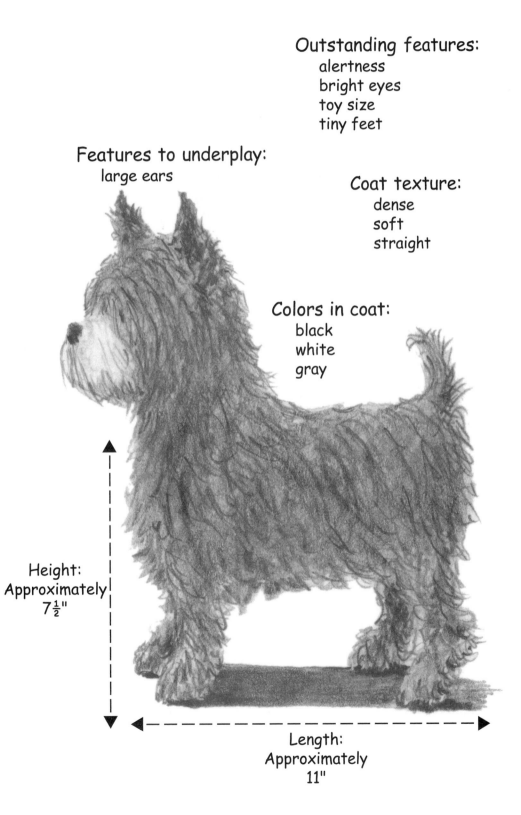

Height:
Approximately
$7\frac{1}{2}$"

Length:
Approximately
11"

Makeover #1
Bandit's Papillon Cut

Equipment:

- Slicker Brush
- Comb
- Clipper
- #10 blade
- #40 blade to use with the
- 3/8" (#2) snap on comb
- Thinning Shears
- Curved Scissor
- Straight scissor
- Nail Trimmer

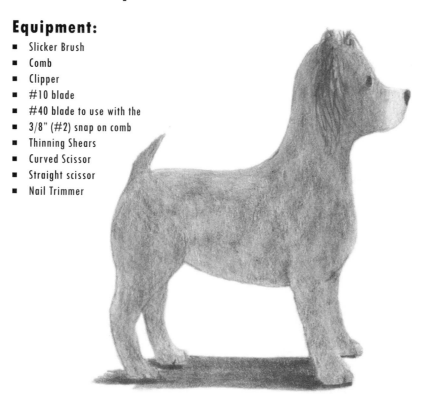

In this makeover I'm going to take advantage of Bandit's oversized ears and play them up with a Papillon ear style. I'm giving his body a short Pet Puppy Cut, with a clean face, short head, and a carrot tail.

Body: Using a #3/8" (#2) snap on comb clip from the back of the skull to the base of the tail and all around the body.

Legs & Feet: Continue clipping with the #3/8" (#2) snap on comb down the legs, picking up each leg and clipping over the foot. Round the feet.

Head & Ears: Using a #10 blade clip the muzzle to the outside eye corners. Using a 3/8" (#2) snap on comb clip the top of the head and the cheeks, blending from the muzzle. Do not clip or scissor any of the long hair on the ears, let it flow and give it a butterfly appearance.

Tail: Trim the underside of the tail with thinning shears to approximately 1–1½".

Makeover #2
Bandit's Sassy Cairn Look

Equipment:
- Slicker Brush
- Comb
- Clipper
- #10 blade
- Thinning Shears
- Curved Scissor
- Straight scissor
- Nail Trimmer

For a totally different look, try a Cairn style. Here I thin Bandit out and shape him, shave his ears and round his head with thinning shears. Remember, Cairns are supposed to be scruffy looking.

Body: Use thinning shears to thin out the body. Make 2–3 cuts, starting close to the skin and working out. Cut a small to medium section at a time. Make the coat length shorter on the back getting gradually longer for the skirt. Thin out until you achieve the desired look.

Legs & Feet: With your thinning shears, continue to thin out until you achieve the shape and length you desire in proportion to the body. Round the feet.

Head & Ears: Using a #10 blade clip both sides of the ears and scissor the edges to the leather. Round the head with straight or curved scissors leaving the ear tips showing above the circle. When you have the desired shape, go over the edges with your thinning shears to give it a more natural appearance.

Tail: Still using thinning shears, shape the tail into a carrot shape approximately 1–2" at the base, depending on the dog's coat length.

Makeover #3
Bandit as a Scotty

Equipment:

- Slicker Brush
- Comb
- Clipper
- #7F
- #10 blade
- Thinning Shears
- Curved Scissor
- Straight Scissor
- Nail Trimmer

This is one of my favorite looks for Bandit. He's not a perfect specimen of dog but a mixture of Miniature Schnauzer, Pomeranian and Chihuahua. I know that with Pomeranian and Miniature Schnauzer in the mix, its safe to say his coat can be grown out to a pretty good length. I've chosen a Scotty look to take advantage of his big ears and color. To make him appear less leggy, we'll let his skirt and legs grow as long as we can.

Body: Using a #7F blade clip from the back of the skull to the base of the tail. Bring the clippers straight down the sides from the elbow to just below the rectum. Do not go under the body. Blend where it's needed with thinning shears and leave the skirt length.

Legs & Feet: Round the feet and let the legs grow.

Head & Ears: Using a #7F blade clip the top of the head, forming a "V" for the eyebrows. Clip between the ear and the outside eye corners. With a #10 blade clean under the eyes, along the sides of the face and down the front of the neck to the Adam's apple forming a "U" or necklace. Next clip the outer and inner ear leaving a fringe on the inside bottom half edge of the ear and out of the ear canal. To set the pattern for the ear tuft length, bend the ear leather in half backwards and smooth the tuft and fringe up to the fold, cut across. Scissor between the brows and sharply triangulate them. Comb the beard length forward.

Tail: Using a #7F blade clip the top and the sides of the tail. Comb the bottom fringe downward and scissor it short from the lower edge of the tail to wide at the base and tapering up to the tip.

Makeover #4
Bandit the Affenpinscher

Equipment:
- Slicker Brush
- Comb
- Clipper
- #10 Blade
- #40 Blade to use with the
- #¾" Snap on comb
- Thinning Shears
- Curved Scissor
- Straight Scissor
- Nail Trimmer

Next we'll be styling Bandit into a modified Affenpinscher. The Affenpinscher and Brussels Griffon look would both work to take advantage of Bandit's cute little "monkey face" and small body. We'll be making an Affenpinscher this time but we could just as easily make him into a Brussels Griffon just by shortening the coat and smoothing him out.

Body: Using a #¾" snap on comb clip from where the neck connects to the body and continue to the base of the tail. Make another stroke on each side of the first to widen the area. The rest of the clipped area of the body will be done with the snap on comb pointing straight down to the table. This blends the clipped area of the body into the skirt. Continue clipping straight down the sides to leave a skirt and do not go under the body. Scissor the skirt very short angling it from the brisket up to the loin tuck up.

Legs & Feet: Round the feet. Pipe the front legs and moderately angulate the back legs.

Head & Ears: Use thinning shears to clean the stop area. Using a #10 blade clip both sides of the ears and neaten the edges with scissors. With curved scissors, round the top of the head from ear to ear leaving the ear tips peeking out. Blend from the occiput into the neck. The neck length will be a little longer than the body length. Neaten the muzzle and jaw line and scissor the circle up behind the ears.

Tail: Scissor it into a modified carrot tail proportionate with the body length, approximately ½–¾" length at the tail base.

Makeover #5
Chinese Crested
Powder Puff Bandit

Equipment:

- Slicker Brush
- Pin Brush
- V Rake
- Comb
- Clipper
- #10 Blade and/or
- #15 Blade
- Thinning Shears
- Curved Scissor
- Nail Trimmer

With the Pomeranian and Miniature Schnauzer in his background, we can achieve some pretty good coat length. His very large ears and small size will come in very handy and even though his tail stands up instead of dropping, he'll be an absolutely enchanting Chinese Crested Powder Puff!

Body: While leaving the length, thin out the coat if necessary. Using thinning shears making 2–3 cuts, starting close to the skin and working out. Cut a small to medium section at a time. Part the coat from the base of the skull to the base of the tail. **Hint**: To help the coat stay parted, using thinning shears, cut up and under the hair on each side of the part and take a couple of snips at the base.

Legs & Feet: Leave the length and thin out if necessary. Round the feet in proportion to the body. Neaten with thinning shears.

Head & Ears: Using a #15 blade clean the muzzle using the outside eye corners as the pattern line. Form an inverted "V" at the stop. Clip down the throat to the Adam's apple to form a "U" or "necklace." Leave the length on top of the head and comb it back. Allow the hair on the ears to be long and flowing. Neaten with thinning shears.

Tail: Leave the length. Neaten with thinning shears.

Makeover #6
Bandit's "Utility Do"

Equipment:

- Slicker Brush
- Comb
- Clipper
- #10 Blade
- #40 Blade to use with the
- 3/8" (#2) Snap on comb
- Curved Scissor
- Straight Scissor
- Nail Trimmer

Remember, as the stylist, you're trying to please the owners, but still make the dogs look the best they can. The last style we're going to put on Bandit is an easy "Utility Do" that will make him look just like a puppy and is so easy to care for.

Body: Using a #3/8" (#2) snap on comb clip from the base of the skull to the base of the tail and all around the body.

Legs & Feet: Continue clipping with the #3/8" (#2) snap on comb down the legs, picking up each leg and clipping over the foot. Round the feet.

Head & Ears: Using the #3/8" (#2) snap on comb clip the head, face and ears. Neaten the edges.

Tail: Scissor into a short carrot tail proportionate with the body, approximately 1–1½" at the base.

Eddie

I'd like you to meet Eddie. I've always looked forward to Eddie and his Mom coming into the shop. He's got eyes that seem like there's got to be a person in there.

Breeds that Eddie Most Resembles

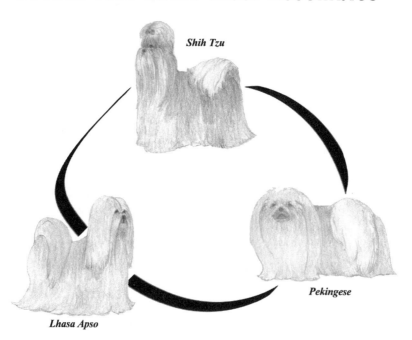

Shih Tzu

Lhasa Apso

Pekingese

EDDIE'S
First Visit Evaluation Notes

Outstanding features:
markings
large eyes
color

Features to underplay:
"windmill ears"

Coat texture: dense, soft, and straight

Colors in coat: black,
white, gray

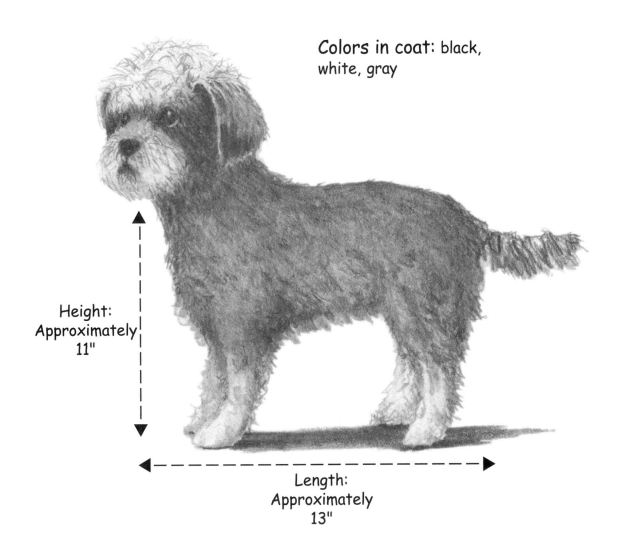

Height:
Approximately
11"

Length:
Approximately
13"

Makeover #7
Eddie's Pet Puppy Cut

Equipment:

- Slicker Brush
- Comb
- Clipper
- #10 Blade and/or
- #40 Blade to use with the
- #1 Snap on Comb
- Thinning Shears
- Curved Scissor
- Straight Scissor
- Nail Trimmer

Talk about "puppy love," this style gives Eddie a soft, cuddly, stuffed animal appearance. We'll make his body and legs all one length, with a round head and fluffy tail.

Body: Using a #1 snap on comb clip from the base of the skull to the base of the tail and all around the body.

Legs & Feet: Continue clipping with the #1 snap on comb down the legs, picking up each leg and clipping over the foot. Round the feet.

Head & Ears: Use the #1 snap on comb and clip the top of the head and the sides of the face. With the thinning shears trim the bangs blending them down into the sides of the face. With curved scissors continue scissoring the circle to the underside of the beard in proportion to the head. Leave the ear length but even them with thinning shears.

Tail: Trim the underside of the tail with thinning shears to approximately 3½–4".

Equipment:
- Slicker Brush
- Pin Brush
- V Rake
- Comb
- Clipper
- #10 Blade
- Thinning Shears
- Curved Scissor
- Straight Scissor
- Nail Trimmer

Makeover #8
Elegant Eddie

Here Eddie is in full coat in contrast to his introduction drawing where his coat is short. When I first evaluated him, I explained to his Mom that Eddie had Shih Tzu, Lhasa Apso and Pekingese in his breed mix, all of which are long coated breeds. Even though a full coat is a lot of maintenance, it's a very doable look.

Body: Leaving the length, thin out if necessary by using thinning shears. Make 2–3 cuts, starting close to the skin and working out. Cut a small or medium section at a time. Part the coat from the base of the skull to the base of the tail.

Legs & Feet: Leave the length and thin out if necessary. Round the feet.

Head & Ears: Scissor the inside eye corners. Leave the length on the head, beard and ears. Part down the center of the top of the head.

Tail: Leave the length and thin out if necessary.

Cleo

Cleo is a sweet older dog. She's been a friend and client of mine for many years. I know where she got her endearing personality from: Her Mom is just as sweet. Like kids, dogs "learn what they live."

Breeds that Cleo Most Resembles

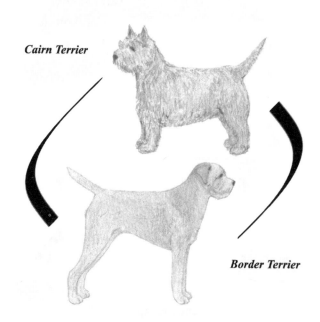

Cairn Terrier

Border Terrier

CLEO'S
First Visit Evaluation Notes

Outstanding features:
markings
soft appealing look
color

Features to underplay:
overweight

Colors in coat:
black
tan

Coat texture:
coarse
straight
soft, undercoat

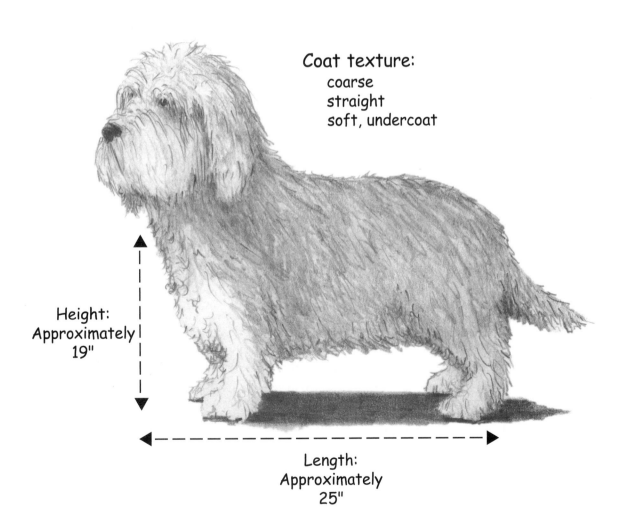

Height:
Approximately
19"

Length:
Approximately
25"

Makeover #9
Cleo—The Perfect PBGV

Equipment:

- Slicker Brush
- Comb
- Clipper
- #10 Blade
- #40 Blade to use with the
- #5/8" Snap on Comb
- #1 Snap on Comb
- Thinning Shears
- Curved Scissor
- Straight Scissor
- Nail Trimmer

Let's make Cleo into a PBGV—Petit Basset Griffon Vendeen—a merry dispositioned dog with a carefree appearance. Sounds like our Cleo. This look will perfectly match Cleo's personality.

Body: Using a #1 snap on comb clip from the base of the skull to the base of the tail. Make another stroke on each side of the first to widen the area. The rest of the clipped area of the body will be done with the snap on comb pointing straight down to the table. This blends the clipped area of the body into the skirt. Continue clipping straight down the sides to leave a skirt and do not go under the body.

Legs & Feet: Even the legs with thinning shears. Round the feet.

Head & Ears: Using #5/8" snap on comb clip the top of the head leaving a visor. Use thinning shears to trim the visor and the inside eye corners, leaving a scruffy look, blend into the neck. Round the end of the ear feathers.

Tail: Using a #1" snap on comb clip all around the tail.

Chester

Look at this guy. Isn't he great? When I look at Chester I have to smile because I am envisioning him in all sorts of hair-do's. Take a look. What would you do with him?

Breeds that Chester Most Resembles

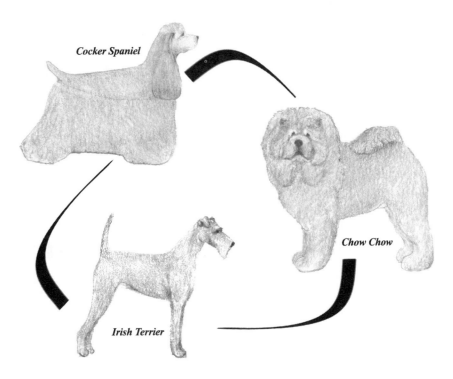

Cocker Spaniel

Chow Chow

Irish Terrier

CHESTER'S
First Visit Evaluation Notes

Outstanding features:
    black tongue
    soft & cuddly coat

Features to underplay:
    stout body
    large head

Colors in coat:
    cream with black

Coat texture:
    thick undercoat
    straight
    soft

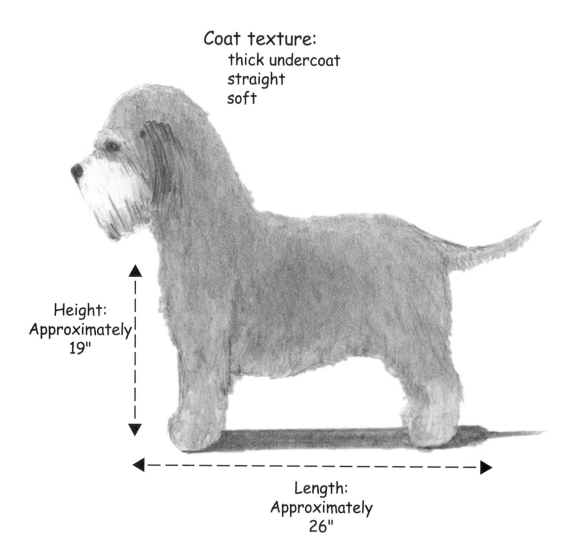

Height:
Approximately
19"

Length:
Approximately
26"

Makeover #10
Chester as a Wheaten

Equipment:
- Slicker Brush
- Comb
- Clipper
- #10 Blade
- #5F Blade
- #40 Blade to use with the
- #3/8" (#2) Snap on Comb and
- #5/8" Snap on Comb
- Thinning Shears
- Curved Scissor
- Straight Scissor
- Nail Trimmer

Chester has the perfect coat to make him into a Soft Coated Wheaten Terrier. Make his legs look longer with a short angled skirt. What better way to elongate and make his head look more proportionate?

Body: Using a #5/8" snap on comb clip from the base of the skull to the base of the tail. Make another stroke on each side of the first to widen the area. The rest of the clipped area of the body will be done with the snap on comb pointing straight down to the table. This blends the clipped area of the body into the skirt. Continue clipping straight down the sides and do not go under the body, blending the body into the skirt and legs. Scissor the skirt short with thinning shears angling from the brisket to the tuck up of the loin.

Legs & Feet: Round the feet. Pipe the front legs and scissor the back legs following the angles.

Head & Ears: Use a #3/8" (#2) snap on comb over approximately two-thirds of the back skull, starting in front of the ear and continuing to the occiput. Blend the hair on the back of the skull into the hair on the neck with thinning shears. Continue down the sides of the face behind the outer eye corner and beneath the ear with the #3/8" (#2) snap on comb. Let the rest fall forward down the nose. Use a #5F blade on the top of the ear and scissor the edge of the leather to neaten.

Tail: Using a #5/8" snap on comb clip all around the tail tapering it to a point on the end.

Makeover #11
Chester as a PWD

Equipment:
- Slicker Brush
- Comb
- Clipper
- #10 Blade
- Thinning Shears
- Curved Scissor
- Straight Scissor
- Nail Trimmer

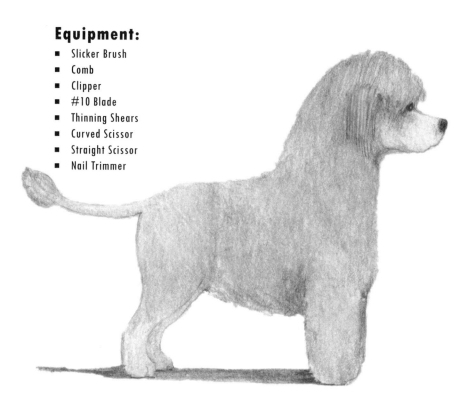

Chester's Mom says it's alright to be creative so, let's deal with Chester's large head by putting him in a lion clip.

Body: Using a #10 blade, clip, starting from the last rib to and including the hindquarters.

Legs & Feet: Continue clipping with the #10 blade down the back legs and feet. Pipe the front legs. Round the feet.

Head & Ears: Using the #10 blade clip all of the muzzle to the outer eye corner. Use thinning shears over the eyes leaving the rest natural.

Tail: Using the #10 blade clip all around the tail from the base towards the tip. Clip about three-quarters of the tail (in proportion to the tail) leaving a plume on the tip end.

Makeover #12
Chester the Schnauzer

Equipment:
- Slicker Brush
- Comb
- Clipper
- #10 Blade
- #7F Blade
- #3/8" (#2) Snap on Comb
- Thinning Shears
- Curved Scissor
- Straight Scissor
- Nail Trimmer

In this makeover let's give Chester's large head the illusion of it being smaller by shaping it like a Schnauzer. To continue the illusion, let's make him look taller and thinner by accenting the skirt tuck up at the loin.

Body: Using a #7F blade clip from the base of the skull to the base of the tail. Make another stroke on each side of the first to widen the area. The rest of the clipped area of the body will be done with the blade pointing straight down to the table. This blends the clipped area of the body into the skirt. Continue clipping straight down the sides to leave a skirt and do not go under the body. Scissor the skirt very short but accent the brisket and tuck up. Blend the sides if needed.

Legs & Feet: Continue using the #7F blade and clip down the back half of the rear legs to a point just above the hock and then shape the fringe over the stifle (knee). Pipe from the hocks down on the back legs and all of the front legs. Round the feet.

Head & Ears: Using a #7F blade clip the top of the head forming a "V" for the brows. Continue with the same blade and clip between the ears and the outside eye corners. Clean under the eyes with a #10 blade, along the sides of the face and down the front of the neck to the Adam's apple forming a "U" or "neck-lace." Scissor between the eyebrows then triangulate them. Continue using the #7F blade clipping the top of the ears and a #10 blade inside them. Scissor them to the edge of the leather to neaten. Comb the beard forward.

Tail: Using a #3/8" (#2) snap on comb clip all around the tail. Use thinning shears to create a fox tail shape.

Oliver

This is Oliver, a precocious Cockapoo. His coloring and markings are just outstanding. Teaming that with his size makes him just about perfect. But don't worry, if you mess up on a mutt, you can always change the whole style a little or all the way. Nothing is wrong!

Breeds that Oliver Most Resembles

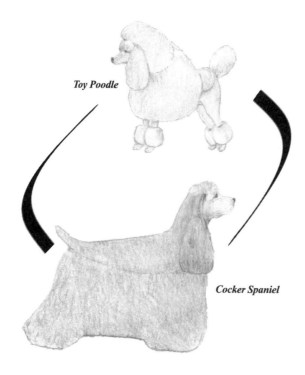

Toy Poodle

Cocker Spaniel

OLIVER'S
First Visit Evaluation Notes

Outstanding features:
small size
soft and cuddly
color

Features to underplay:
soft coat mats easily
long legs for the body

Colors in coat:
black
tan

Coat texture:
curly
soft

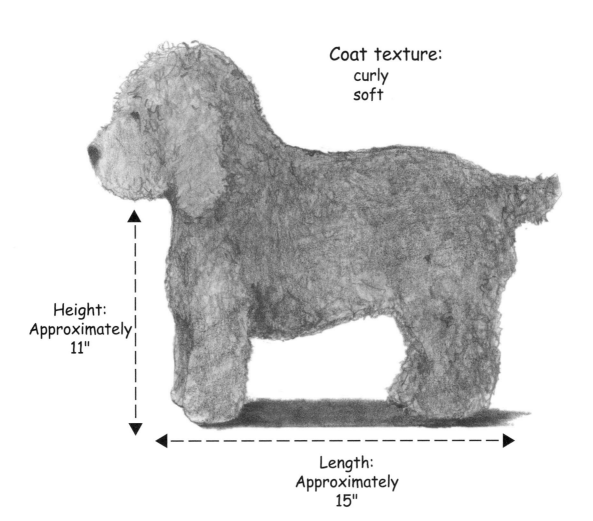

Height:
Approximately
11"

Length:
Approximately
15"

134

Makeover #13
Oliver in a modified Bichon Frise Cut

Equipment:
- Slicker Brush
- Comb
- Clipper
- #10 Blade
- Curved Scissor
- Straight Scissor
- Nail Trimmer

We're taking advantage of Oliver being so soft and huggable just like a live teddy bear. This cut will require more frequent brushings to keep him nice between stylings. The best thing to do in this situation is to educate Oliver's Mom on proper brushing techniques.

Body: Using your straight scissors trim the coat to approximately 2" all over. Start at the base of the tail pointing toward the neck and continuing down the sides. Accent the brisket by working up to the loin tuck up.

Legs & Feet: Round the feet. Pipe all four legs using straight scissors, pointing straight down from the shoulder to the table and around to create a cylindrical shape. Repeat this same process only from the hip on the back legs. Use curved scissors to bevel each foot.

Head & Ears: Keeping the body proportion in mind, round the head into a modified Bichon head. With the convex side of the curved scissor—the high side of the curve—pointing away from the dog, scissor in front of the eyes at the stop. Round the top of the head, going over the skull, ear to ear. Shorten the ears at the bottom edge almost to the leather and while rounding the sides of the face, incorporate the ears into the circle by beveling the bottoms. Continue the circle by rounding the beard in proportion to the rest of the head.

Tail: Scissor the tail in proportion to the body length.

Makeover #14
Oliver as a Mini Cocker

Equipment:
- Slicker Brush
- Comb
- Clipper
- #10 Blade
- #7F Blade
- Curved Scissor
- Straight Scissor
- Nail Trimmer

This is my favorite creative look for Oliver. Picture this little cutie as a Cocker Spaniel with a crown on his head to accent his tan eyebrows. His ear feather texture is perfect. Even though Oliver's coat is curly, the weight you'll get as his coat gets longer will make the curl wavy instead. Now, let's see how adorable he'll look.

Body: Use a #7F blade from the base of the skull to the base of the tail. Make another stroke on each side of the first to widen this area. The rest of the of the clipped area of the body will be done with the clipper blade pointing straight down to the table. This blends the clipped area of the body into the skirt. Continue straight down the sides to leave a skirt. Do not go under the body. Blend the clipped sides into the skirt with thinning shears where it is needed and neaten the bottom edge of the skirt.

Legs & Feet: Round the feet and let the legs flow down as they grow.

Head & Ears: Use a #10 blade on the back two-thirds of the head, the top one-third of the ears (inside and out), the face and down the throat to the Adam's apple forming a "U" or "necklace." Trim the clipped edges of the ears with straight scissors and blend the front one-third top of the head (crown) into the back two-thirds of the head with thinning shears.

Tail: Use a #10 blade all around it.

Makeover #15
Oliver in a Modified Poodle Kennel Clip with a Moustache

Equipment:

- Slicker Brush
- Comb
- Clipper
- #10 Blade
- #40 Blade to use with the
- #¾" Snap on Comb
- Curved Scissor
- Straight Scissor
- Nail Trimmer

This is more like a variation on a Poodle look. I'm not going to give Oliver shaved Poodle feet for three reasons. First, it will detract from Oliver's naturally cute and cuddly look. Second, his coat texture is just soft enough that it will appear too limp on his legs. Finally, it would make his legs appear longer. Because Oliver is a male, I decided not to give him a Poodle tail but to make it the same length as the rest of his body. For the same reason, I'll give him a little donut moustache.

Note: If Oliver was a female, I would give her a pompon tail and refrain from giving her a moustache for a much softer and more feminine look.

Body: Using a #¾" snap on comb clip from the base of the skull to the base of the tail and all around the body.

continued...

Makeover #15
Oliver in a Modified
Poodle Kennel Clip—cont'd.

Legs & Feet: Round the feet and blending down from the body, pipe all four legs. The back legs will appear slightly angulated because of the softness of the coat.

Head & Ears: Using a #10 blade starting from underneath the ear, clip to the eye corners and then under the eye. Continue clipping following the lip line halfway to the nose leaving the rest for a small donut or moustache. Clipping the top of the nose from this point to the eyes only, forming an inverted "V" between the eyes. Clip down the throat to the Adam's apple forming a "U" shape or a "necklace."

Form the topknot by brushing it forward from the base of the skull and scissor a circle. Use the stop, the top of the ears and the base of the skull as your pattern. Repeat a circle, brushing back and side to side. Scissor the circle four times in all. Fluff up and even it out.

When rounding the donut, proportion it to the body. Leave the ear length.

Tail: Using a #¾" snap on comb clip all around it.

Jane

The first time I met Jane, though she was absolutely gorgeous, her previous groomer had shaved her down completely. This infuriated her Mom. Jane has exceptional coloring and markings, because she has Cocker Spaniel, English Springer Spaniel, and Standard Poodle in her breed mix. I know that her coat will grow back beautifully. Let's see how we can best show her off now!

Breeds that Jane Most Resembles

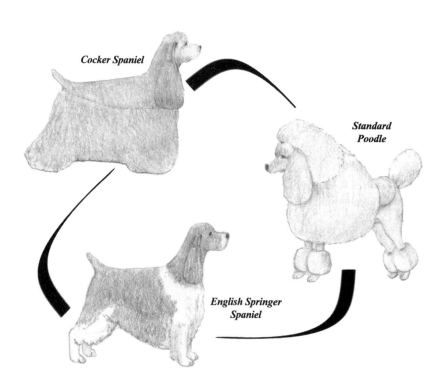

Cocker Spaniel

Standard Poodle

English Springer Spaniel

JANE'S
First Visit Evaluation Notes

Outstanding features:
markings
coloring
proportions

Features to underplay:
legs a little too long

Colors in coat:
tan
black

Coat texture:
wavy
soft

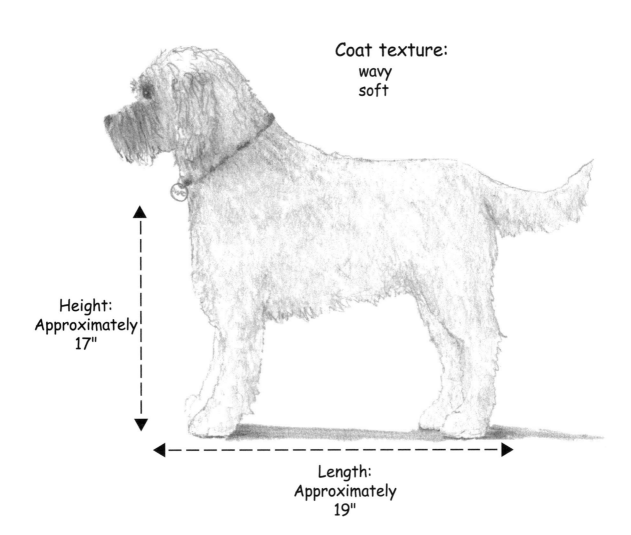

Height:
Approximately
17"

Length:
Approximately
19"

Makeover #16
"Jane Cocker"

Equipment:

- Slicker Brush
- Comb
- Clipper
- #10 Blade
- Thinning Shears
- Curved Scissor
- Straight Scissor
- Nail Trimmer

With her ears, coat and coloring, won't Jane be a terrific Giant Cocker Spaniel? She'll be so striking "strutting her stuff."

Body: Using a #10 blade starting at the base of the skull clip to the base of the tail. Make another stroke on each side of the first to widen this area. The rest of the clipped area of the body will be done with the clipper blade pointing straight down to the table. This blends the clipped area of the body into the skirt. Continue clipping straight down the sides to leave a skirt. Do not go under the body. Blend the clipped sides into the skirt with thinning shears.

Legs & Feet: Round the feet into a large circle to let the legs flow down into a bell bottom.

Head & Ears: Using a #10 blade clip the back two-thirds of the head, the top one-third of the ear (inside and out), the face and down the throat. Trim the clipped edges of the ears with straight scissors and blend the front one-third top of the head (crown) into the back two-thirds of the head with thinning shears.

Tail: Trim the underside of the tail to approximately 4–4½".

Makeover #17
Jane in a PWD Working Retriever Clip

Equipment:

- Slicker Brush
- Comb
- Clipper
- #4F Blade
- #5F Blade
- #10 Blade
- #40 Blade to use with the
- #3/8"(#2) Snap on Comb
- #1 Snap on Comb
- Thinning Shears
- Curved Scissor
- Straight Scissor
- Nail Trimmer

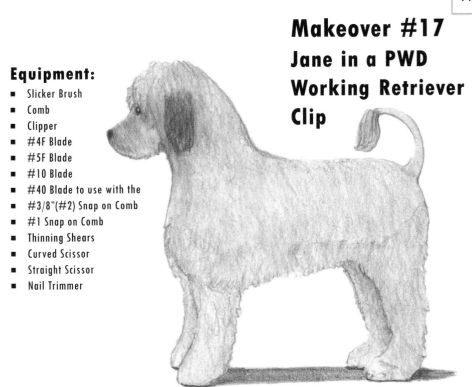

Jane is the perfect size (17–23") and has the perfect wavy coat to make her a Portuguese Water Dog. Did you know the AKC has two accepted grooming styles for the Portuguese Water Dog? We'll put Jane in one of them—the Working Retriever Clip. Do you see why knowing your breeds is imperative?

Body: Using a #1 snap on comb clip from the base of the skull to the base of the tail and all around the body.

Legs & Feet: Pipe the front legs and angulate the back legs in proportion to the body length (approximately 1" long). Round the feet.

Head & Ears: Using a #4F blade clip only the muzzle back to the outer eye corners. Trim the stop area with thinning shears. Clip the topknot with the #1 snap on comb so it will blend with the body coat. Bevel the bangs above the eyes to make them appear deep set.

Clip the hair on the ears with a #3/8" (#2) snap on comb on the outside and a #10 blade on the inside. Use straight scissors to trim the edge of the ear leather.

Tail: Using a #5F blade clip two-thirds of the tail leaving the last one-third in a natural plume.

Makeover #18
Jane Of the Jungle

Equipment:

- Slicker Brush
- Comb
- Clipper
- #10 Blade
- #7F Blade
- Curved Scissor
- Straight Scissor
- Nail Trimmer

Jane in a Lowchen's lion clip is a daring but very feasible makeover. Here's why: Jane's breed mix includes a Standard Poodle, an English Springer Spaniel and a Cocker Spaniel. We know that the Poodle's coat can grow to as much as 8" in length and Springer's and Cocker's can grow long too, so coat length will not be a problem. Her wavy and soft coat texture lends itself perfectly to this styling.

Body: Using a #7F blade clip from the last rib to and including the hindquarters, leaving the front full and natural.

Legs & Feet: Continue clipping with the #7F blade to halfway down the hock joint on the back legs. Clip the front legs from the elbow to a point above the knee matching the height of the back cuffs. Round the feet but leave the cuff length natural.

Head & Ears: Scissor the inside eye corners, scissoring to a point at the stop. Allow the hair on the top of head to part and flow to the sides. Let all the length other than the inside eye corners flow naturally.

Tail: Using the #7F blade clip all around the tail and halfway to the tip leaving the plume natural.

Makeover #19
Jane as a Poodle

Equipment:

- Slicker Brush
- Comb
- Clipper
- #4F Blade
- #5F Blade
- #7F Blade
- #10 Blade
- #30 Blade
- #40 Blade to use with the
- #3/8"(#2) Snap on Comb
- Thinning Shears
- Curved Scissor
- Straight Scissor
- Nail Trimmer

Since Jane is part Poodle, let's bring it out in this makeover. We'll shave her face to give her topknot the illusion of being fuller. I'll even give Jane pantaloons and Poodle feet. With her coloring, this style will be very eye catching.

Body: Using a #7F blade clip from the base of the skull to the base of the tail and all around the body cutting around the pattern for the pantaloons (refer to page 74).

Legs & Feet: Using a #30 blade shave Poodle feet (refer to page 74). Scissor the front and back legs approximately 1½", scissoring the pantaloons to blend into the leg length.

Head & Ears: Using a #10 blade to clean the face and using the outer eye corners as the pattern, take the clippers straight back to underneath the ears. Shave the muzzle and clip the throat down to the Adam's apple to form a "U" or a "necklace." Brush the topknot forward from the base of the skull and scissor a circle using the stop, to the top of the ears and the base of the skull as your pattern. Repeat the circle, brushing it back and then from side to side, scissoring the circle four times. Fluff up and even it. With a #10 blade, clip the top one-third of the ear leather inside and out. Trim the shaved edges with straight scissors and curve the bottom of the ear feathers with curved scissors.

Tail: Trim the underside of the tail with thinning shears to approximately 4".

Makeover #20
Jane as an English Springer Spaniel

Equipment:
- Slicker Brush
- Comb
- Clipper
- #10 Blade
- #7F Blade
- Thinning Shears
- Curved Scissor
- Straight Scissor
- Nail Trimmer

Since Jane appears to have some Springer in her background, let's bring it out. She's the right size, and I have no doubt that we can grow out her coat and ears. We'll just have to deal with her long tail by giving it a Golden Retriever style.

Body: Using a #7F blade clip from the base of the skull to the base of the tail. Make another stroke on each side of the first to widen the area. The rest of the clipped area of the body will be done with the clipper blade pointing straight down to the table. This blends the clipped area of the body into the skirt. Leave the chest full from the top of the breastbone to the front of the shoulder bone and down.

Legs & Feet: Continue using the #7F blade on the top and the sides of the front legs from the top of the leg and stopping at the ankle. Let the fringe on the back of the legs grow, neatening with thinning shears. Pull the hair up from between the toes and scissor to the contour of each whole foot and the toes. Round the feet. On

continued...

Makeover #20
Jane as an English Springer Spaniel—cont'd.

the back legs, lift the leg featherings up and clip all around the legs from the hock joint to the ankle using the #7F blade. For the back feet, repeat the same process as the front feet.

Head & Ears: Using a #10 blade clip the top of the head, the face and down the throat to the Adam's apple forming a "U" or "necklace." Continue clipping with the #10 blade on the top one-third of the ear both inside and out, scissoring the clipped edges to neaten.

Tail: Scissor the bottom feathers tapering from a point at the tip to very wide at the base. Go back over the bottom edge with thinning shears to give a more natural appearance.

Mitty

Every time I see Mitty I want to scoop him up in my arms and just hold him tight. I keep telling his Mom that I would take him home in a second, but she won't part with him. I understand completely.

Breeds that Mitty Most Resembles

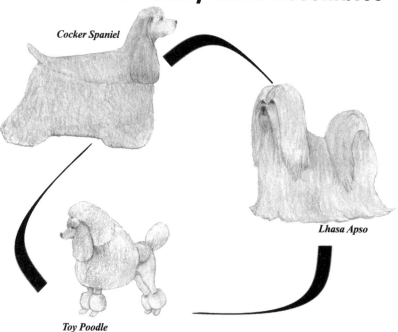

Cocker Spaniel

Lhasa Apso

Toy Poodle

MITTY'S
First Visit Evaluation Notes

Outstanding features:
adorable face
size

Features to underplay:
slew feet on front

Colors in coat:
black
tan

Coat texture:
medium coarse
wavy
soft undercoat

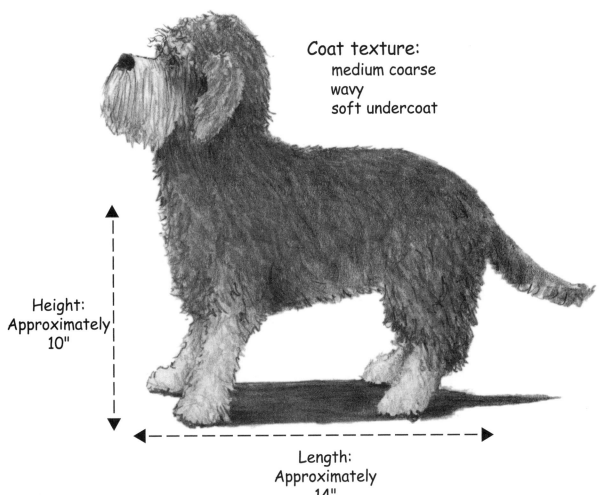

Height:
Approximately
10"

Length:
Approximately
14"

Makeover #21
Mitty's Pet Puppy Cut

Equipment:

- Slicker Brush
- Comb
- Clipper
- #10 Blade
- #40 Blade to use with the
- #5/8" Snap on Comb
- Curved Scissor
- Straight Scissor
- Nail Trimmer

With his Border Terrier face, a Pet Puppy Cut will be a good style for Mitty. This makeover is easily adaptable for summer by removing more of the coat length, and winter by letting the coat length grow out. This is accomplished by changing the size of the snap on comb attached to the clipper blade that is used to give the cut. Pet Puppy Cuts aren't necessarily the same length of coat all the time but the length chosen for the coat should be used on the body and legs.

Body: Using a #5/8" snap on comb clip from the base of the skull to the base of the tail and all around the body.

Legs & Feet: Continue clipping with the #5/8" snap on comb down the legs, picking up each leg and clipping over the foot. Round the feet.

Head & Ears: Continue clipping with the #5/8" snap on comb on top of the head, leaving enough for a small visor and the top of the ear leather. Clip the inside ear leather with a #10 blade. Scissor the ears to the leather and curve the beard from the front to the outside eye corner. Shape a short visor over the eyes.

Tail: Neaten the tail but leave its length.

Equipment:
- Slicker Brush
- Comb
- Clipper
- #10 Blade
- #7F Blade
- #4 Skip Tooth Blade
- Thinning Shears
- Curved Scissor
- Straight Scissor
- Nail Trimmer

Makeover #22
Mitty Becomes Royalty

Let's try something really daring and different. Let's give Mitty a modified Cavalier King Charles Spaniel look. His ears won't be quite so long and elegant and his face will be a little longer but Mitty's coat is medium coarse and wavy and the Lhasa Apso in him will make it possible to grow it out to a good length.

Body: Using a #4 skip tooth blade clip from the base of the skull to the base of the tail. Make another stroke on each side of the first to widen the area. The rest of the clipped area of the body will be done with the clipper blade pointing straight down to the table. This blends the clipped area of the body into the skirt. Continue clipping straight down the sides creating a long skirt. Do not go under the body. Blend with thinning shears where it is necessary.

Legs & Feet: Using a #7F blade clip the top and the sides of the front legs from the top and stopping at the ankle. Leave the foot fluffy, creating slippers, and let the fringe on the back of the leg grow into feathers. On the back legs follow the stifle with thinning shears leaving approximately ¾". Where the stifle's curve ends and the leg straightens, continue clipping with the #7F blade straight down on the front and the two sides, stopping at the ankle leaving the foot fluffy and the hocks feathered. Lightly round the outer edges of each foot.

Head & Ears: Using a #10 blade clip the top of the head and the face. Do not go under the neck. Blend into the neck. The ears will probably only grow to half a CKCS length but keep allowing the ears to grow and neaten the bottoms with thinning shears.

Tail: Allow it to grow out to a long and flowing length.

Makeover #23
Mitty as a Havanese

Equipment:

- Slicker Brush
- Pin Brush
- V Rake
- Comb
- Clipper
- #10 Blade
- Thinning Shears
- Curved Scissor
- Straight Scissor
- Nail Trimmer

The Lhasa Apso in Mitty is going to allow me to get enough coat length and waviness so that I can grow him into a cute Havanese. He's the perfect size and the Havanese can be any color. We're going to give him braids on each side of the head to keep the hair out of his eyes. His tail won't flip up over his back and his ear feather won't be quite so full but I will let them grow out as much as possible. This style will perfectly cover the fact that he has slew feet.

Body: Leaving the length, thin out if necessary by using thinning shears. Make 2–3 cuts, starting close to the skin and working out. Cut a small to medium section at a time. Part the coat from the base of the skull to the base of the tail.

Legs & Feet: Leave the length and thin out if necessary.

Head & Ears: Scissor the inside eye corners. Part down the center of the top of the head. Section off three braid strands on each side using head hair only. Braid each side starting loosely so the braid will lay and tighten it up as you go. Use a small latex band to secure each braid.

Tail: Let the tail grow and flow naturally. Neaten with the thinning shears if necessary.

Makeover #24
Dandy Dinmont Mitty

Equipment:

- Slicker Brush
- Comb
- Clipper
- #10 Blade
- #7F Blade
- #5F Blade
- Thinning Shears
- Curved Scissor
- Straight Scissor
- Nail Trimmer

Did you see a Dandie Dinmont when you looked at Mitty the first time? The charm of the Dandie Dinmont Terrier is the exaggerated size of his head and great big eyes. He's a little tall but we can work with that. Ready for the renovation?

Body: Using a #5F blade clip starting two fingers-width from the base of the skull to the base of the tail. Make another stroke on each side of the first to widen the area. The rest of the clipped area of the body will be done with the clipper blade pointing straight down to the table. This blends the clipped area of the body into the skirt. Continue clipping straight down the sides to leave a skirt. Do not go under the body. Make the skirt 1½"– 2" long from the brisket to the loin tuck up with thinning shears. Blend the sides into the skirt with thinning shears.

continued...

Makeover #24
Dandy Dinmont Mitty—cont'd.

Legs & Feet: Continue clipping with the #5F blade straight down the back half of the rear legs to a point just above the hocks. Shape the fringe with curved scissors to curve with the stifle (knee) and with straight scissors pipe from the hock down. Pipe the front legs with straight scissors. Round and bevel the feet with curved scissors.

Head & Ears: Scissor clean around the eyes, the stop and the top of the nose to make the eyes appear as large as possible. Brush the topknot forward from the base of the skull and even it off across the front, softly framing the eyes by extending the bangs over the eye slightly. Fluff up and continue scissoring around the head slightly extending over the ears and skull. Keep scissoring until you get the appearance of a large chrysanthemum (rounded, high and fluffy). Thin the cheeks out and down. Tassel the ears starting by lifting the overflowing topknot and using a #7F blade clipping down the leather leaving the feathers in an inverted "V" at the bottom of the ear. Shape

continued...

Makeover #24
Dandy Dinmont Mitty—cont'd.

the bottom of the tassel on each ear to a distinct point with thinning shears. Scissor the shaved edges of the ear leather to neaten. Shape the beard straight across the bottom with thinning shears to proportion.

Tail: Scissor the tail with thinning shears in the shape of a sickle.

Cameo

Cameo hits the shop door wagging her tail and half of her back-side. Her coat is versatile and looks terrific in all three of her makeovers.

Breeds that Cameo Most Resembles

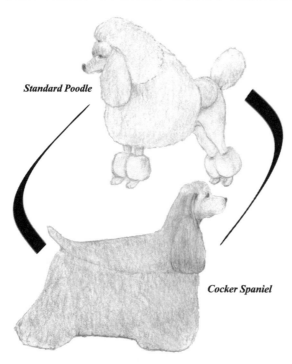

Standard Poodle

Cocker Spaniel

CAMEO'S
First Visit Evaluation Notes

Features to underplay:
    shallow stop
    neck too long
    head too small
    overweight
    long feet

Outstanding features:
    silky ears
    rich color
    friendly

Colors in coat:
    buff

Coat texture:
    almost silky
    wavy
    soft

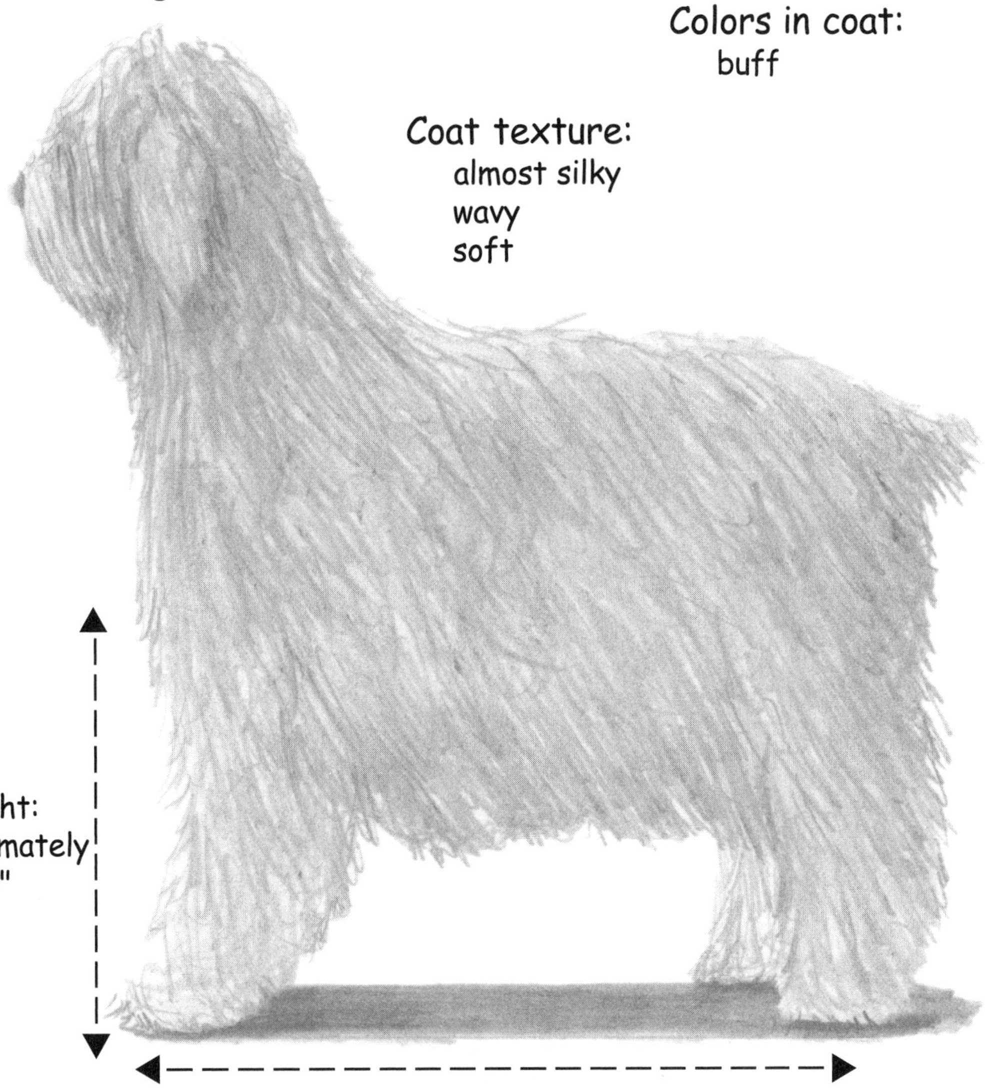

Height:
Approximately
20"

Length:
Approximately
28"

Makeover #25
Cameo the Friendly Briard

Equipment:

- Slicker Brush
- Pin Brush
- Comb
- Clipper
- #10 Blade
- Thinning Shearss
- Curved Scissor
- Straight Scissor
- Nail Trimmer

Cameo's coat has a slight wave to it and the coloring is close to that of a Briard, so let's try that look. For an even better reason though, we'll use this style to downplay many of Cameo's problem features including: a long neck, overweight, a shallow stop, small head size, feet that are too long, and "toothpick legs." Yes, this will work perfectly!

Body: Leaving the coat length thin out if necessary by using thinning shears to make 2–3 cuts, starting close to the skin and working out. Cut a small to medium section at a time. Part the coat from the base of the skull to the base of the tail.

Legs & Feet: Leave the length and thin out if necessary. Round the feet leaving them large and full.

Heads & Ears: Scissor the inside eye corners. Leave the hair length on the head, beard and ears. Part down the center of the top of the head. **Note**: You also have the option to put a topknot, pigtails or nubs on the head (refer to page 52).

Tail: Leave the length. Neaten with thinning shears if necessary.

Makeover #26
Cameo as an Old English Sheepdog

Equipment:

- Slicker Brush
- Pin Brush
- V Rake
- Large Comb
- Clipper
- #10 Blade
- #1 Snap on Comb
- Thinning Shears
- Curved Scissor
- Straight Scissor
- Nail Trimmer

In this makeover, we'll grow out her coat then make her body coat just a little shorter and her legs a little longer. Doing so will offset her weight and "toothpick legs." Even though her coat texture is mostly silky, soft, and wavy we can still make it work because her body is so large that it will compensate for the coat lying closer. She's the same general size and even though she has a stub of a tail, she will make a great blonde Old English Sheepdog!

Body: Using a #1 snap on comb clip from the base of the skull to the base of the tail and all around the body.

Legs & Feet: Let the legs continue to grow and round the feet in proportion to her leg length.

Head & Ears: Continue to grow out, rounding and keeping it in proportion to the body.

Tail: Scissor the tail to the same length as the body all around.

Makeover #27
Cameo All Mixed Up

Equipment:
- Slicker Brush
- V Rake
- Comb
- Clipper
- #10 Blade
- #40 Blade to use with the
- #¾" Snap on Comb
- #½" Snap on Comb
- Curved Scissor
- Straight Scissor
- Nail Trimmer

By mixing different styles and matching what looks the best on Cameo, in this "mixed up makeover" we will enhance her good features while covering up the bad ones. She has a small head in proportion to the rest of her body, her neck is too long and she has very little stop, but she has beautiful silky ears, lending itself perfectly to a modified Bichon head. She's an overweight dog so we'll use a #½" snap on comb on her body and tail to make her appear thinner. It will also give her soft wavy coat a velvety appearance and give her short tail the opportunity to be seen wagging.

Body: Use a #½" snap on comb clip from the base of the skull to the base of the tail and all around the body.

Legs & Feet: Round the feet and scissor all four legs to approximately 2" in length. By scissoring her toothpick legs to 2–3" and rounding her long feet, this will give her legs a bell bottom look.

continued...

Makeover #27
Cameo All Mixed Up—cont'd.

Head & Ears: Fluff all of the head including the face and ears. Scissor straight across in front of the eyes at the stop. Round the top of the head, going over the skull ear to ear. Leave the ears full but rounding the ends. Continue rounding the circle on the sides and the bottom of the beard in proportion to rest of the body.

Tail: Using a #¾" snap on comb clip all around the tail.

Reba

Reba has a great disposition. She also has just the right combination of breeds in her background to take creativity to its limits and come up with some pretty nifty styling.

Breeds that Reba Most Resembles

Giant Schnauzer

Standard Poodle

REBA'S
First Visit Evaluation Notes

Outstanding features:
    silky ears
    rich color
    friendly

Features to underplay:
    shallow stop
    neck too long
    head too small
    overweight
    long feet

Colors in coat:
    dark gray
    black

Coat texture:
    wavy
    soft

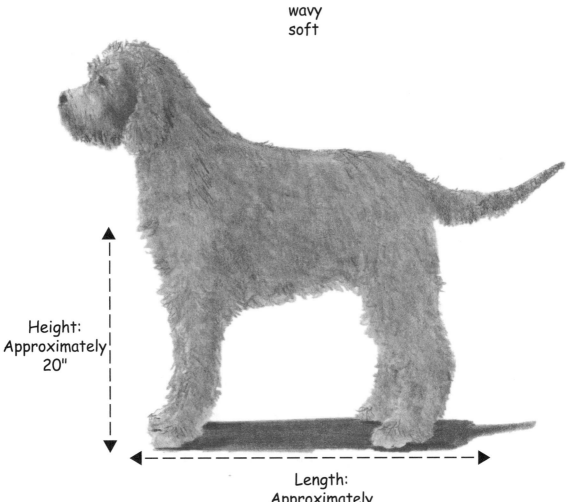

Height:
Approximately
20"

Length:
Approximately
28"

Makeover #28
Reba as a Kerry Blue/ Wheaten

Equipment:
- Slicker Brush
- Comb
- Clipper
- #5F Blade
- #10 Blade
- #40 Blade to use with the
- #3/8" (#2) Snap on Comb
- Thinning Shears
- Curved Scissor
- Straight Scissor
- Nail Trimmer

Reba's color and size immediately makes me think of a Kerry Blue Terrier. Now, all we have to do is to modify the rest of her. But because her coat is straighter, make the body more like a Soft Coated Wheaten, trim her tail and shave her ears and we have a "Wee Kerry."

Body: Using a #3/8" (#2) snap on comb clip from the base of the skull to the base of the tail. Make another stroke on each side of the first to widen the area. The rest of the the clipped area of the body will be done with the snap on comb pointing straight down to the table. This blends the clipped area of the body with the skirt. Continue clipping straight down the sides. Do not go under the body. Next, blend the body into the skirt and legs with thinning shears. Scissor the skirt short with thinning shears angling from the brisket to the tuck up of the loin.

Legs & Feet: With curved scissors round the feet. Pipe the front legs and angulate the back legs with straight and curved scissors. The feet will stick out a little because of the coat texture.

Head & Ears: Using a #5F blade clip the top of the head clip a "V" above the brows. Do not scissor between them. This hair will flow forward down the nose forming the fall. Comb the eyebrows forward, point the thinning shears toward the nose, keeping the points away from the eye, and trim the brows just over the eyes to make the eyes visible. With a #10 blade, clip from underneath the ear to the inside corner of the eye, cleaning under the eye, and down the throat to the Adam's apple forming a "U" or a "necklace." Using a #5F blade clip the top of the ears, a #10 blade inside the ear and scissor them to the leather.

Tail: Trim the underside of the tail with thinning shears approximately 3–3½".

Makeover #29
Reba as an
Irish Water Spaniel

Equipment:

- Slicker Brush
- Comb
- Clipper
- #10 Blade
- #40 Blade to use with the
- #1 Snap on Comb
- Thinning Shears
- Curved Scissor
- Nail Trimmer

What a neat look! Reba isn't brown but she is dark gray/black and since she's a mutt, that will work. She's has the right size and even though her coat isn't curly, it is thick and wavy. Her tail will look great as a rat tail as will her head with it's natural overflowing topknot and clean face. We'll cover her feet with longer leg coat.

Body: Using a #1 snap on comb clip from the base of the skull to the base of the tail and all around the body.

Legs & Feet: Pipe the front legs and angulate the back legs scissoring the length to approximately 1¾"–2". Round the feet.

Head & Ears: Using a #10 blade clip around the muzzle and underneath the ear using the outside eye corner as your pattern line. Continue down the throat to just below the Adam's apple forming a "U" or "necklace." Scissor the topknot letting it overflow the eyes, ears and occiput. Shape the ears with curved scissors leaving them full and natural (use thinning shear on the bottoms if necessary for a more natural appearance).

Tail: Divide the tail into thirds. Using the #10 blade clip the bottom two-thirds to the tip. Blend the top one-third into the body by making it the same length.

Makeover #30
Reba as a Bearded Collie

Equipment:
- Slicker Brush
- Pin Brush
- V Rake
- Comb
- Clipper
- #10 Blade
- Thinning Shears
- Curved Scissor
- Straight Scissor
- Nail Trimmer

Although this is a high maintenance style let's grow Reba out into a full coat. Mom will have to brush her daily or bring her for grooming weekly, but won't she be elegant?

Body: Using thinning shears thin out the body by making 2–3 cuts, starting close to the skin and working out. Cut a small to medium section at a time. Keep thinning out until the coat lies nicely. Part the coat from the base of the skull to the base of the tail.

Legs & Feet: Still using your thinning shears, continue thinning out. Round the feet.

Head & Ears: Clean the inside eye corners. Thin out until the coat lies nicely. Leave the ear length long. Part the hair on the top of the head. **Note**: You also have the option to put a topknot, pigtails or nubs on the head. (Refer to page 52.)

Tail: Leave the tail length long.

Makeover #31
Reba as a Portuguese Water Dog

Equipment:
- Slicker Brush
- Comb
- Clipper
- #10 Blade
- Thinning Shears
- Curved Scissor
- Straight Scissor
- Nail Trimmer

Reba is going to get herself a Lion Clip. A black lion. Too cool! Let's get started!

Body: Using a #10 blade clip the body starting from the last rib to and including the hindquarters.

Legs & Feet: Continue clipping with the #10 blade down the back legs and the feet. Round the feet. Pipe the front legs.

Head & Ears: Continue clipping with the #10 blade on all of the muzzle to the outer eye corner, just past the lips. Scissor with thinning shears over the eyes leaving the rest natural.

Tail: Using the #10 blade clip all around the tail halfway to the tip leaving the plume on the end natural.

Tyke

Tyke is one of the most fortunate of dogs. He was adopted by a lady who not only adores him but also takes the best care of him. Tyke visits me every four weeks and then visits McDonald's afterwards for his treat. We should all be treated so well.

Breeds that Tyke Most Resembles

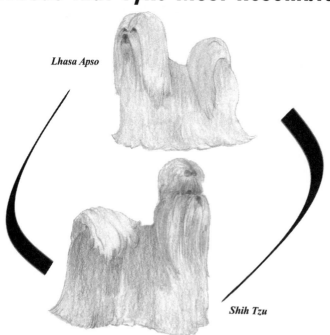

Lhasa Apso

Shih Tzu

TYKE'S
First Visit Evaluation Notes

Outstanding features:
loveable face
great big eyes

Features to underplay:
coat mats easily

Colors in coat:
shades of buff

Coat texture:
thick
soft

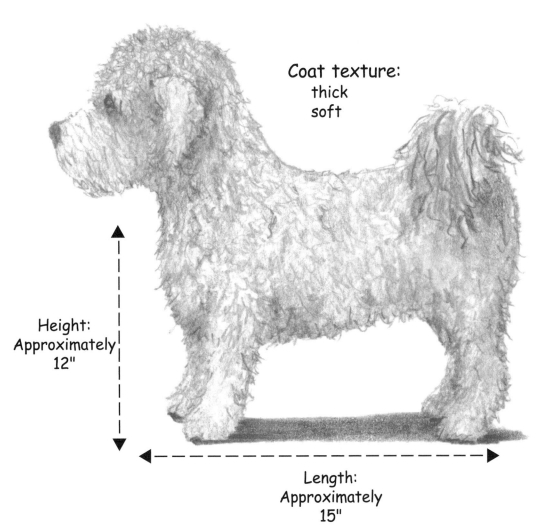

Height:
Approximately
12"

Length:
Approximately
15"

Makeover #32
Tyke as an Irresistable Bichon

Equipment:
- Slicker Brush
- Comb
- Curved Scissor
- Straight Scissor
- Nail Trimmer

Let's try making Tyke over as a Bichon Frise. He's just about the right size, with a coat texture similar to that of a Bichon and he has a flip tail too.

Body: Using your straight scissors, trim the coat to approximately 2" all over. Start at the base of the tail pointing toward the neck and continuing down the sides. Accent the brisket to the loin tuck up.

Legs & Feet: Round the feet and pipe all four legs.

Head & Ears: Keeping body proportion in mind, round the head into a modified Bichon head. With the convex side of the curved scisssors—the high side of the curve—pointing away from the dog, scissor in front of the eyes at the stop. Round the top of the head, going over the skull, ear to ear. Shorten the ears at the bottom edge almost to the leather and while rounding the sides of the face, incorporate the ears into the circle by beveling the bottoms. Continue the circle by rounding the beard in proportion to the rest of the head.

Tail: Scissor the tail in proportion to the body length, approximately 4½–5".

Makeover #33
Tyke as a PWD
in a Retriever Clip

Equipment:

- Slicker Brush
- Comb
- Clipper
- #10 Blade
- #7F Blade
- #5F Blade
- #40 Blade to use with the
- #¾" Snap on Comb
- #3/8" (#2) Snap on Comb
- Thinning Shears
- Curved Scissor
- Straight Scissor
- Nail Trimmer

Tyke is shorter than the PWD and not the right color but since he's a mutt and we have no standards to hamper our creativity, let's make him a Miniature Portuguese Water Dog. You'll like it trust me!

Body: Use a #¾" snap on comb from the base of the skull to the base of the tail and all around the body.

Legs & Feet: Pipe the front legs and angulate the back legs in proportion to the body length approximately ¾–1" long. Round the feet.

Head & Ears: Use the #5F blade to clip the muzzle only back to the outer eye corners. Trim the stop area with thinning shears. Scissor the top of the head across the skull ear to ear. Continue curving down into the ear without separating from the topknot. Bevel the bangs above the eyes to make them appear deep set. Clip the hair on the ears with a #3/8" (#2) snap on comb on the outside and a #10 blade on the inside. Use straight scissors to trim the edge of the ear leather.

Tail: Using a #7F blade clip two-thirds of the tail leaving the last one-third in a natural plume.

Makeover #34
Tyke as a
Dandy Dinmont

Equipment:
- Slicker Brush
- Comb
- Clipper
- #5F Blade
- #7F Blade
- #10 Blade
- Thinning Shears
- Curved Scissor
- Straight Scissor
- Nail Trimmer

Okay! So, Tyke's body isn't as long as a Dandie's but that's the point of this book. Make the best out of what you have and utilize your assets! Tyke has the head and eyes for a Dandie Dinmont Terrier so let's start with that. His legs are too long and body too short for a Dandie which gives us a choice of just giving Tyke a Pet Puppy Cut or counter the difference with a little "mutt magic," which is what we'll do here. Tyke's legs are too long for this cut, so we'll shorten the topside and lengthen the underside. Let's elongate the brisket and not make the tuck-up so severe. We'll also make the circumference of the legs a little larger. From there we'll give the illusion of length by making the chest and backside of the rump longer. Now this is really creative styling!

continued...

Makeover #34
Tyke as a Dandy Dinmont—cont'd.

Body: Using a #7F blade starting two fingers-width down the neck clip from the base of the skull to the base of the tail. Make another stroke on each side of the first to widen the area. The rest of the clipped area of the body will be done with the clipper blade pointing straight down to the table. This blends the clipped area of the body into the skirt. Continue clipping straight down the sides to leave a skirt. Do not go under the body. The rest will blend out to approximately 2" long except the chest and the rump, which will be left as long as proportionately possible. When shortening the skirt, bring it approximately halfway down the front legs and angle it gently to the loin with thinning shears. Blend the clipped sides into the skirt with thinning shears.

Legs & Feet: Round the feet. Pipe the front legs to approximately 2". Be sure to make them long enough in the front to blend with the chest length. Angulate the back legs accenting and leaving the rump hair as long as you can to create the illusion of body length. Scissor the front of the back legs shorter but accent the curve of the stifle.

Head & Ears: Clean under the eyes, stop and top of the nose to make the eyes appear as large as possible. Brush the topknot forward from the base of the skull and even it off across the front, softly framing the eyes by extending the bangs over the eyes slightly. Fluff up and continue scissoring around the head slightly extending over the ears and skull. Keep scissoring until you get the appearance of a large chrysanthemum, rounded, high and fluffy. Thin the cheeks out and down. Tassel the ears by lifting the overflowing topknot and with a #7F blade clip down the leather leaving the feathers in an inverted "V" at the bottom of the ear. With thinning shears, shape the bottom of the tassel to a distinct point. Scissor the shaved edges of the ear leather to neaten. Shape the bottom of the beard straight with thinning shears to proportion.

Tail: Scissor the tail with thinning shears in the shape of a sickle.

Fred

Fred has been my friend for a dozen or so years and with all good friendships we've been through both easy and hard times. Back in the 90's, Fred was hit by a car and blinded. Not only was he courageous but his Mom was too. She spent a lot of time and patience working with Fred to cope with his new life. The two of them were a total success. I'm so proud to be their friend.

Breeds that Fred Most Resembles

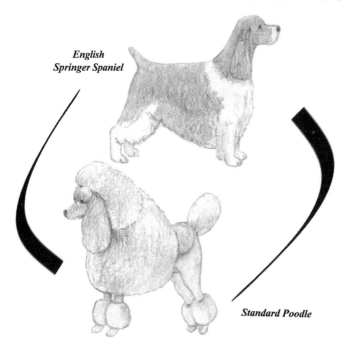

English Springer Spaniel

Standard Poodle

FRED'S
First Visit Evaluation Notes

Outstanding features:
good proportions
sweetness

Features to underplay:
a little overweight
coat mats easily

Colors in coat:
blonde with black
highlighting

Coat texture:
thick
straight
soft

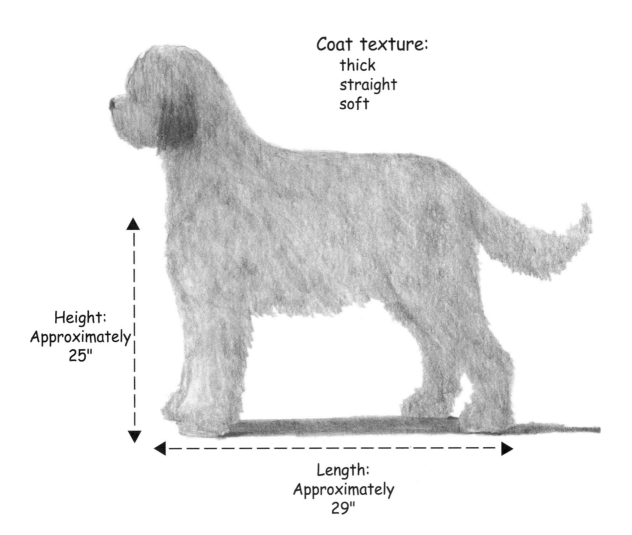

Height:
Approximately
25"

Length:
Approximately
29"

Makeover #35
Fred All Mixed Up

Equipment:
- Slicker Brush
- Comb
- Clipper
- #10 Blade
- #40 Blade to use with the
- #3/8" (#2) Snap on Comb and
- #1 Snap on Comb
- Curved Scissor
- Straight Scissor
- Nail Trimmer

Fred will always be a puppy to me. So, let's make him look like one. We'll make the coat on his body a little shorter than his legs to offset his weight. This will also hide his "toothpick legs." Along with a modified Bichon head and a little off his tail he'll be just perfect.

Body: Using a #3/8" (#2) snap on comb clip from the base of the skull to the base of the tail and all around the body.

Legs & Feet: Using a #1 snap on comb down the legs, blend at the body, and picking up each leg clip over the foot. Round the feet.

Head & Ears: Keeping body proportion in mind, round the head into a modified Bichon head. Fluff the head and face and scissor straight across the front of the eyes at the stop. Round the top of the head, going over the skull, ear to ear. Continue the circle by rounding the sides of the face and beard in proportion to the rest of the head and the body. Leave the ears a little longer than the beard and round the bottoms.

Tail: Trim the underside of the tail with thinning shears to approximately 4–4½".

Makeover #36
King Fred the First

Equipment:
- Slicker Brush
- Comb
- Clipper
- #10 Blade
- #7F Blade
- Thinning Shears
- Curved Scissor
- Straight Scissor
- Nail Trimmer

Let's try a variation of the "Lion Clip." We're going to do the Lowchen's lion trim with a full and natural mane, a lion tail and we'll give Freddie cuffs. He's going to be so regal.

Body: Using a #7F blade clip from the last rib to and including the hindquarters, leaving the front full and natural.

Legs & Feet: Continue the #7F blade clipping to halfway down the hock joint on the back legs. Clip the front legs from the elbow to a point above the knee matching the height of the back cuffs. Round the feet but leave the cuff length natural.

Head & Ears: Scissor the inside eye corners, scissoring to a point at the stop. Allow the top of the head hair to part and flow to the sides. Let all the hair length other than the inside eye corners flow naturally.

Tail: Using the #7F blade clip all around the tail halfway to the tip leaving the plume natural.

Lucy & Pogo

As you can see I've combined Lucy's and Pogo's makeover pages. Standing side by side you would see little Lucy as a "miniature mutt" and Pogo as a "standard mutt." As with the Schnauzer, their styles can be interchanged.

Breeds that Lucy & Pogo Most Resemble

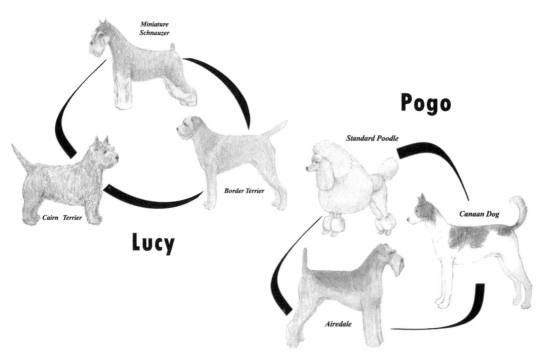

Miniature Schnauzer

Pogo

Standard Poodle

Cairn Terrier

Border Terrier

Canaan Dog

Lucy

Airedale

LUCY & POGO'S
First Visit Evaluation Notes

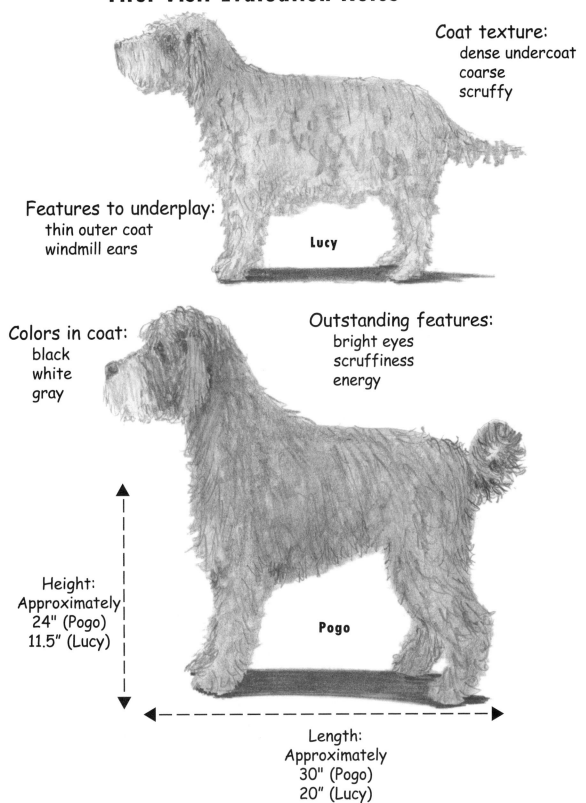

Coat texture:
  dense undercoat
  coarse
  scruffy

Features to underplay:
  thin outer coat
  windmill ears

Lucy

Colors in coat:
  black
  white
  gray

Outstanding features:
  bright eyes
  scruffiness
  energy

Pogo

Height:
Approximately
24" (Pogo)
11.5" (Lucy)

Length:
Approximately
30" (Pogo)
20" (Lucy)

Makeover #37
Wirehaired Pointing Griffon
Pogo

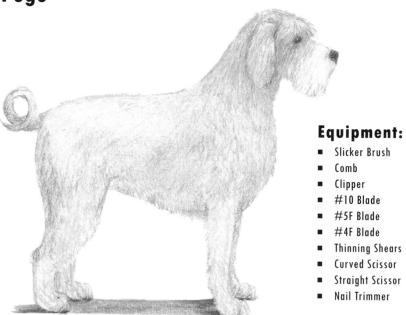

Equipment:
- Slicker Brush
- Comb
- Clipper
- #10 Blade
- #5F Blade
- #4F Blade
- Thinning Shears
- Curved Scissor
- Straight Scissor
- Nail Trimmer

In this makeover, we'll give Pogo a Wirehaired Pointing Griffon look. She's got the right size, proper coat, and she has the head and beard for it. Although she's not exactly the right color with her grizzled gray with liver coming through, she's dark. The dead give away that Pogo is a mutt is her signature curly tail. Keep in mind that Lucy too can be made into a mini Wirehaired Pointing Griffon.

Body: Using a #4F blade clip from the base of the skull to the base of the tail and all around the body.

Legs & Feet: Continue clipping with the #4F blade down the legs, picking each foot up and clipping over the foot. Round each foot.

Head & Ears: Using the #5F blade clip the top of the head leaving enough hair to form eyebrows in a "V" shape. Continue clipping the sides of the face from the outer eye corners to underneath the ears, leaving the beard. Scissor between the eyebrows, then triangulate them. Leave the beard length, scissoring straight across then neatening with thinning shears.

Tail: Using a #4F blade clip all around the tail.

Makeover #38
Airedale Pogo
King of the Terriers

Equipment:

- Slicker Brush
- Comb
- Clipper
- #10 Blade
- #7F Blade
- Thinning Shears
- Curved Scissor
- Straight Scissor
- Nail Trimmer

Pogo has Airedale in her background anyway. She's about the same size and even though she doesn't have button ears that half stand up, she does have "windmill ears." That will create a similar illusion. We can grow her face out into a fall. She's a solid color. As with the previous makeover we put her in, the Wire Haired Pointing Griffon Pogo, her tail will be her signature.

Body: Using a #7F blade clip from the base of the skull to the base of the tail. Make another stroke on each side of the first to widen the area. The rest of the clipped area of the body will be done with the clipper blade pointing straight down to the table. This blends the clipped area of the body into the skirt. Continue clipping straight down the sides to create a small skirt. Do not go under the body. Work from the elbow to curve up and over the hip. Neatly angle the bottom of the skirt from the brisket up to the loin tuck up with thinning shears.

Legs & Feet: Round the feet with curved scissors. Pipe the front legs and angulate the back legs in proportion to the body length with straight and curved scissors.

Head & Ears: Using a #7F blade clip the top of the head leaving enough hair to form eyebrows in a "V" shape. Leave the hair between the eyes to form the fall. Clip with the #7F blade on the top of the ears. Continue clipping with the #7F blade between the outside eye corners and inside the ears. With thinning shears clean the inside eye corners. With straight scissors, triangulate the eyebrows short and trim around the ear edges with curved scissors, shape the beard into a barrel shape.

Tail: Continue clipping with the #7F blade and clip all around the tail.

Makeover #39
Pogo the Canaan Dog

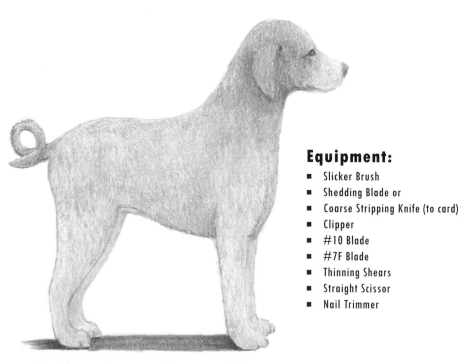

Equipment:

- Slicker Brush
- Shedding Blade or
- Coarse Stripping Knife (to card)
- Clipper
- #10 Blade
- #7F Blade
- Thinning Shears
- Straight Scissor
- Nail Trimmer

Looking at Pogo's tail I suspect Pogo is part Canaan Dog. Let's pretend that she's a pure-bred with only a couple of mutt issues. Her drop ears are her big draw back from her Canaan Dog's disguise being perfect, but other than that, she's the right size, and her color is acceptable because Canaan's can be solid colors with or without a small amount of white too.

Body: Using a #7F blade clip from the base of the skull to the base of the tail and all around the body.

Legs & Feet: Continue clipping with a #7F blade down the legs, picking up each leg and clipping over the foot. Round the feet.

Head & Ears: Using a #10 blade clip the muzzle to underneath the ears. Then clip down the throat to the Adam's apple forming a "U" or "necklace." Clip all of the ear, inside and out, and then scissor the edges to neaten. Clip the top of the skull with the #10 blade and use thinning shears to blend it into the neck if needed.

Tail: Shorten and neaten the tail with thinning shears in proportion to the body approximately 1½–2" long.

Makeover #40
Pogo as a
Border Terrier

Equipment:
- Slicker Brush
- Comb
- Clipper
- #10 Blade
- #4F Blade
- Curved Scissor
- Straight Scissor
- Nail Trimmer

Even though she's a little big, Pogo will look good as a Border Terrier. Her coat will be perfect for this style. We'll keep her body and legs short and give her a Border Terrier face.

Body: Using a #4F blade clip from the base of the skull to the base of the tail and all around the body.

Legs & Feet: Continue clipping with the #4F blade down the legs, picking up each leg and clipping over the foot. Round the feet.

Head & Ears: Using the #4F blade clip the top of the head leaving enough for a small visor. Curve the beard from the front to the outside eye corner and shape the visor short. Leave the ear length.

Tail: Continue clipping with the #4F blade all around the tail.

Makeover #41
Lucy as a Border Terrier Too

Equipment:
- Slicker Brush
- Comb
- Clipper
- #10 Blade
- #4F Blade
- Thinning Shears
- Curved Scissor
- Nail Trimmer

Lucy could be the perfect Border Terrier too. Her size and build are just right. Even though her tail is a little long and she has "windmill ears" we can make this work to her advantage.

Body: Using a #4F blade clip from the base of the skull to the base of the tail and all around the body.

Legs & Feet: Continue clipping with the #4F blade down the legs, picking up each leg and clipping over the foot. Round the feet.

Head & Ears: Using the #4F blade clip the top of the head leaving enough for a small visor. Curve the beard from the front to the outside eye corner and shape the visor short. Leave the ear length, neatening with thinning shears.

Tail: Continue clipping with the #4F blade all around the tail.

Makeover #42
The "Schnuppy"

Equipment:

- Slicker Brush
- Comb
- Clipper
- #10 Blade
- #40 Blade to use with the
- #1/4" Snap on Comb and
- #3/8" (#2) Snap on Comb
- Curved Scissor
- Straight Scissor
- Nail Trimmer

In this makeover we're going to give Lucy a Schnauzer face with a Pet Puppy Cut body. Picture Pogo in the same cut.

Body: Using a #3/8" (#2) snap on comb clip from the base of the skull to the base of the tail and all around the body.

Legs & Feet: Continue clipping with the #3/8" (#2) snap on comb down the legs, picking up each leg and clipping over the foot. Round the feet.

Head & Ears: Using a #1/4" snap on comb clip the top of the head forming a "V" for the eyebrows. Continue with the same snap on comb on the sides of the face, from the outer eye corners to underneath the ears, leaving a Schnauzer beard and brows. Clean under the eyes with a #10 blade and along the sides of the face and down the neck to the Adam's apple forming a "U' or "necklace." Scissor between the eyebrows, then triangulate them. Leave the ear feather length.

Tail: Leave the tail natural.

Nash

Meet Nash. He was named after the city of Nashville, where he was found wandering around inside a hotel, by his mom and dad while they were on their honeymoon. After several unsuccessful attempts to find Nash's owner, the new couple became a threesome. Lucky dog!

Breeds that Nash Most Resembles

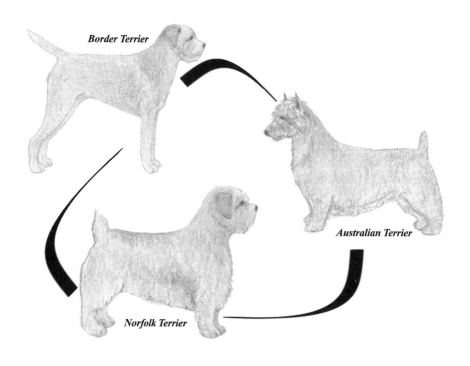

Border Terrier

Australian Terrier

Norfolk Terrier

NASH'S
First Visit Evaluation Notes

Outstanding features:
    coloring
    body proportion

Features to underplay:
    slew feet front and back

Colors in coat:
    brown
    black
    tan

Coat texture:
    harsh
    straight
    soft undercoat

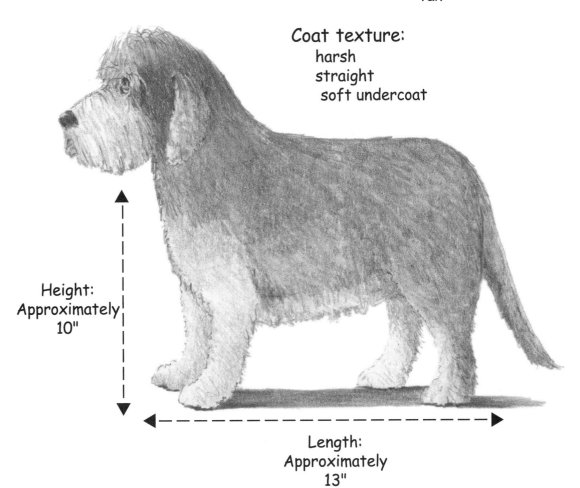

Height:
Approximately
10"

Length:
Approximately
13"

Makeover #43
Nash as an Otterhound Puppy

Equipment:
- Slicker Brush
- V Rake
- Comb
- Clipper
- #10 Blade
- #40 Blade to use with the
- #1¼" Snap on Comb
- Thinning Shears
- Curved Scissor
- Straight Scissor
- Nail Trimmer

Nash has the right colors, the right coat texture, the right body and proportions to be an Otterhound. The only mutt issue we have to work around is his small size but we have the answer to that one too. Everyone loves a puppy and that's just what we'll make Nash into.

Body: Using a #1¼" snap on comb clip from the base of the skull to the base of the tail and all around the body.

Legs & Feet: Using a #1¼" snap on comb clip down the legs, picking up each leg and clipping over the foot. Round the feet.

Head & Ears: Trim the inside eye corners with straight scissors. Continue using the #1¼" snap on comb clip the top of the head and the sides of the face.

Tail: With thinning shears, shape the tail into a fox tail approximately 2–2½" at the base.

Makeover #44
Nash as a Modified
Norfolk Terrier

Equipment:
- Slicker Brush
- Comb
- Clipper
- #10 Blade
- #5F Blade
- #40 Blade to use with the
- #3/8" (#2) Snap on Comb
- Thinning Shears
- Curved Scissor
- Straight Scissor
- Nail Trimmer

Nash will make a great Norfolk Terrier because his color, size and coat texture are perfect. Nash's mutt issues are his long tail and his legs are longer than the Norfolk but when styling mutts everything is relative and nothing is wrong.

Body: Using a #3/8" (#2) snap on comb clip from the base of the skull to the base of the tail. Make another stroke on each side of the first to widen the area. The rest of the clipped area of the body will be done with the snap on comb pointing straight down to the table. This blends the clipped area of the body into the skirt. Continue clipping straight down the sides. Do not go under the body. Neaten the skirt with thinning shears.

Legs & Feet: Leave the leg length, neatening with thinning shears and round the feet with curved scissors.

Head & Ears: Using a #5F blade clip the top of the head leaving just enough hair for very short brows, shortened with thinning shears. Continue between the outside eye corner and underneath the ear blending into the neck. Using a #10 blade clip both sides of the ear and trim around the edges of the leather.

Tail: Using the #3/8" (#2) snap on comb clip all around the tail.

Makeover #45
Nash as a Modified
Sealyham Terrier

Equipment:
- Slicker Brush
- Comb
- Clipper
- #10 Blade
- #7F Blade
- Thinning Shears
- Curved Scissor
- Straight Scissor
- Nail Trimmer

The first thing I see when I look at Nash is a Sealyham Terrier. They are compact little dogs with rectangular heads. Nash's mutt issues include his coloring, a long tail, long legs, and slew feet. I know what we can do to correct these issues but my one concern is knowing Nash doesn't have the coat capabilities to have a long flowing skirt. I know this because his breed mix includes, Border Terrier, Australian Terrier and Norfolk Terrier. Nevertheless, we can probably grow out some furnishings.

Body: Using a #7F blade clip from the base of the skull to the base of the tail. Make another stroke on each side of the first to widen the area. The rest of the clipped area of the body will be done with the clipper blade pointing straight down to the table. This blends the clipped area of the body into the skirt. Continue clipping straight down the sides to leave a skirt. Do not go under the body. Allow the skirt to continue to grow as long as possible only neatening with thinning shears. Blend wherever it is necessary.

Legs & Feet: Allow the hair on the legs to grow as long as possible only neatening with thinning shears. Round the feet with curved scissors.

Head & Ears: Using a #7F blade clip the top of the head leaving enough hair to create a fall and eyebrows. Continue clipping down the sides of the face. Clip down the throat. Using a #10 blade clip both sides of the ears and neaten the ear edges with the straight scissors. Triangulate the eyebrows but do **not** clip between, allowing the fall to flow. Shape the beard with thinning shears leaving it longer in the front.

Tail: Neaten the tail but leave the length.

189

Makeover #46
Nash Impersonates a Schnauzer

Equipment:

- Slicker Brush
- Comb
- Clipper
- #10 Blade
- Thinning Shears
- Curved Scissor
- Straight Scissor
- Nail Trimmer

The Schnauzer cut is always an, "Oldie But Goodie." Nash is a great terrier mix. With his harsh, straight coat and excellent beard and eyebrows, he'll make a great little Schnauzer. In this makeover we will have to address Nash's long tail, and his brown and tan colors are not quite right for a Schnauzer.

Body: Using a #10 blade clip from the base of the skull to the base of the tail. Make another stroke on each side of the first to widen the area. The rest of the clipped area of the body will be done with the clipper blade pointing straight down to the table. This blends the clipped area of the body into the skirt. Continue clipping straight down the sides to leave a skirt. Do not go under the body. Scissor the bottom of the skirt accenting the brisket up to the tuck up.

Legs & Feet: Continue clipping with the #10 blade down the back half of the rear legs to a point just above the hock and then shape the fringe over the stifle (knee). Pipe from the hocks down on the back legs and pipe the front legs with straight scissors. Round the feet with curved scissors.

Head & Ears: Using the #10 blade clip the top of the head forming a "V" for the brows. Continue with the same blade and clip between the ears and the outside eye corners. Clean under the eyes with a a #10 blade, along the sides of the face and down the front of the neck to the Adam's apple forming a "U" or "necklace." Scissor between the eyebrows and triangulate them. Continue clipping using the #10 blade on both sides of the ears and scissor them to the ear leather to neaten. Comb the beard forward.

Tail: Use thinning shears to shorten the tail in proportion to the body approximately 1–1½" long.

Sandy & Sparkey

The only differences between Sandy and Sparkey are their coloring, length of tail, and of course, we can't forget gender. They both have the same coat texture and sweet dispositions.

Breeds that Sandy and Sparky Most Resemble

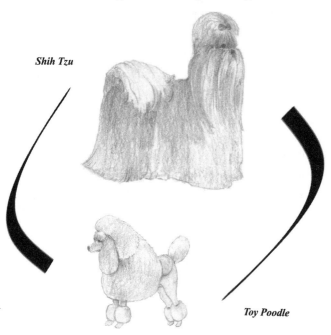

Shih Tzu

Toy Poodle

SANDY & SPARKEY'S
First Visit Evaluation Notes

Outstanding features:
   loveable face
   size
   softness
   color

Features to underplay:
   coat mats easily

Colors in coat:
   Sandy: blonde
   Sparkey: silver, black, gray

Coat texture:
   wavy
   soft

Height:
Approximately
12"

Length:
Approximately
14"

Makeover #47
Blondes Have More Fun

Equipment:
- Slicker Brush
- Comb
- Clipper
- #10 Blade
- #7F Blade
- Thinning Shears
- Curved Scissor
- Straight Scissor
- Nail Trimmer

In this styling we'll give Sandy piped legs with a modified pantaloon top on the back legs. We will also give her a short skirt. We can soften her look by leaving some hair on her head and face. Although Sandy has a short tail and Sparkey has a long tail, with a little "mutt magic," we'll have twins.

Body: Using a #7F blade clip from the base of the skull to the base of the tail. Make another stroke on each side of the first to widen the area. The rest of the clipped area of the body will be done with the clipper blade pointing straight down to the table. This blends the clipped area of the body into the skirt. Continue clipping straight down the sides making sure not go under the body. Cut around the modified pantaloon pattern for the back legs (refer to page 74).

Legs & Feet: Pipe the legs scissoring straight down from the shoulder with straight scissors. Pipe the back legs to match the piped front leg length and scissor the top of the pantaloons to blend into the legs. Round the feet and bevel around the bottoms with curved scissors.

Head & Ears: Using a #7F blade clip the muzzle to the outside eye corners continuing straight back to underneath the ears and down the neck into the body. Brush the topknot forward from the base of the skull and scissor a circle using the stop, the top of the ears and the base of the skull as your pattern. Repeat the circle after brushing it back and then from side to side. Fluff it up and even it. Use a #10 blade to clip the top one-third of the ear, inside and out and neaten the clipped edges with scissors.

Tail: Using a #7F blade clip around the tail.

Makeover #48
A Fancy French Do

Equipment:
- Slicker Brush
- Comb
- Clipper
- #5F Blade
- #10 Blade
- #30 Blade
- Curved Scissor
- Straight Scissor
- Nail Trimmer

Let's give Sandy a totally different look by bringing out the Poodle in her. We'll give her a topknot, clean face, pantaloons and a Poodle tail. Okay, so how could we work this for Sparkey? Even out his tail and give him a donut moustache.

Body: Using a #5F blade clip from the base of the skull to the base of the tail and all around the body cutting around the pattern for pantaloons (refer to page 86).

Legs & Feet: Shave Poodle feet with a #30 blade (refer to page 74). Scissor the front and back legs approximately 1½". Scissor the top of the pantaloons to the leg length (refer to page 74).

Head & Ears: Using a #10 blade clean the face using the outside eye corners as the pattern and take the clippers straight back to underneath the ears. Shave the muzzle then clip down the throat to the Adam's apple to form a "U" or a "necklace." Brush the topknot forward from the base of the skull and scissor a circle using the stop, the tops of the ears and the base of the skull as your pattern. Repeat the circle after brushing it back and then from side to side. Fluff up and even it. Leave the ears full.

Tail: Continue clipping with the #10 blade all around the tail leaving just enough on the end to round out a Poodle pompon. Pull the long hair out, twist a couple of times, then snip it straight off to the desired length. Circle your thumb and forefinger with the hair fluffed out over the top and using curved scissors start scissoring a circle around the bottom of what's resting on your hand. Repeat two more times after pulling your hand up a little more each time. Let go, fluff out and reshape it.

Makeover #49
Sparkey Gets Variety

Equipment:
- Slicker Brush
- Comb
- Clipper
- #10 Blade
- #7F Blade
- Thinning Shears
- Curved Scissor
- Straight Scissor
- Nail Trimmer

Change and variety are said to be the spice of life and we are really going to make things spicy for Sparkey with this styling. Let's give him a Schnauzer body, a Border Terrier face and a fox tail.

Body: Using a #7F blade clip from the base of the skull to the base of the tail. Make another stroke on each side of the first to widen the area. The rest of the clipped area of the body will be done with the clipper blade pointing straight down to the table. This blends the clipped area of the body into the skirt. Continue clipping straight down the side making sure not to go under the body. Leave a very short skirt but be sure to accent the brisket and the tuck up. Blend the sides into the skirt with thinning shears.

Legs & Feet: Continue clipping with the #7F blade down the back half of the rear leg to a point just above the hock joint and shape the fringe over the stifle (knee) with curved scissors. Pipe from the hocks down also piping the front legs with straight scissors. Round the feet with curved scissors.

Head & Ears: Using the #7F blade on top of the head and the ears leaving enough for a small visor. With straight scissors, scissor the ears to the leather's edge and with curved scissors curve the beard from the front to the outside eye corner. Continue with the straight scissor and shape the visor short.

Tail: Using thinning shears shape the tail into a fox tail, approximately 2–2½".

Makeover #50
Sparkey is such a Lamb Chop

Equipment:

- Slicker Brush
- Comb
- Clipper
- #4F Blade
- #10 Blade
- Curved Scissor
- Straight Scissor
- Nail Trimmer

Why not try a modified Bedlington Terrier look for Sparkey? Of course, since it's modified, Sandy could be styled this way too but some of the effect would be lost without a long tail. Let's try and see what happens.

Body: Using a #4F blade clip from the base of the skull to the base of the tail. Make another stroke on each side of the first to widen the area. The rest of the clipped area of the body will be done with the clipper blade pointing straight down to the table. This blends the clipped area of the body into the skirt. Continue clipping straight down the sides to leave a skirt. Do not go under the body. This way you can elongate the brisket and sharply tuck up the loin.

Legs & Feet: With curved scissors round the feet. Pipe the front legs and angulate the back legs with straight and curved scissors.

Head & Ears: Using a #10 blade clip from the corner of the ear to the outside corner of the eye. Continue clipping from the corner of the eye to behind the corner of the mouth. Also clip the entire under jaw continuing down the neck to form a deep "V" just below the Adam's apple. Scissor the head flat on the sides blending it up into a full topknot that is close at the sides and full at the top. Scissor the topknot evenly from the base of the neck to the tip of the nose giving it the lamb appearance. Scissor the muzzle around in proportion to the head. The front view of the head will appear long and straight, arching across the top between the ears. The muzzle tapers slightly. Using a #10 blade clip from the top of the ear (both sides) to the bottom. Scissor the clipped ear leather edges to neaten.

Tail: Divide the tail into thirds. Use a #10 blade to clip the bottom two-thirds to the tip. Blend the top one-third into the body by making them the same length.

Chewey

Chewey certainly is unique. He's a "low rider" and tries so hard to walk around with an attitude that says, "I'm one bad boy," but he's just kidding. He's the sweetest of dogs.

Breeds that Chewey Most Resembles

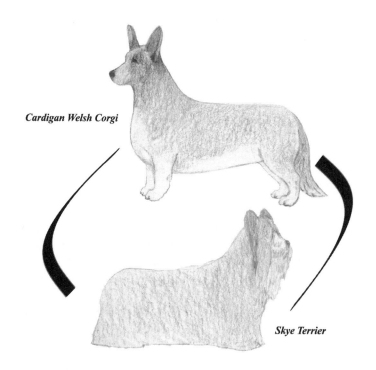

Cardigan Welsh Corgi

Skye Terrier

CHEWEY'S
First Visit Evaluation Notes

Outstanding features:
    dark face
    dark butterfly ears
    soft liquid brown eyes

Colors in coat:
    cream
    black
    tan

Features to underplay:
    guard hairs do not cover legs
    feet too long
    tail coat is thin and scruffy

Coat texture:
    coarse straight guard hair
    massive soft undercoat

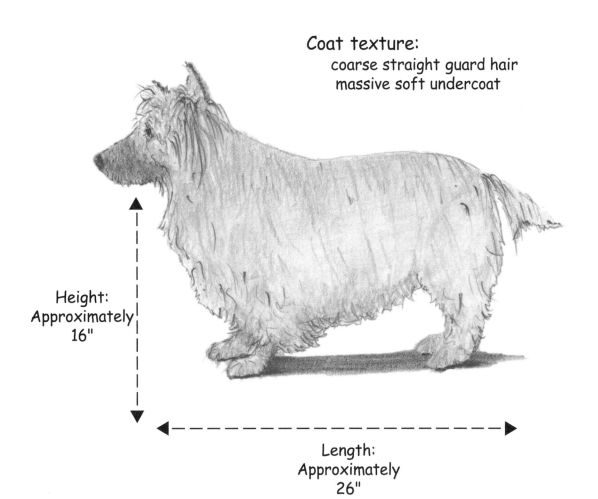

Height:
Approximately
16"

Length:
Approximately
26"

Makeover #51
Chewey Cardigan Welsh Corgi

Equipment:
- Slicker Brush
- V Rake
- Comb
- Clipper
- #10 Blade
- #5F Blade
- Thinning Shears
- Straight Scissor
- Nail Trimmer

This trim will have everyone thinking that Chewey was faking being a mutt this whole time and walking around in disguise. He will become a Cardigan Welsh Corgi thanks to you!

Body: Using a #5F blade clip from the base of the skull to the base of the tail and all around the body.

Legs & Feet: Continue clipping down the legs with the #5F blade. Scissor the feet on the top and the bottom.

Head & Ears: Smooth over the head, face and ears clipping with the #10 blade. Blend into the neck with the thinning shears. Trim around the ear edges with straight scissors.

Tail: Using a #5F blade clip all around the tail.

Makeover #52
Chewey as an Australian Terrier

Equipment:
- Slicker Brush
- Comb
- Clipper
- #10 Blade
- #40 Blade to use with the
- #¾" Snap on Comb
- Thinning Shears
- Curved Scissor
- Straight Scissor
- Nail Trimmer

I can see an Australian Terrier when I look at Chewey. Chewey is certainly bigger, his coloring is too light and his tail does not stand up but he has a coarse coat, stand up ears and a potential "ruff" around his neck. He definitely has the makings of an Australian Terrier with our help.

Body: Using a #¾" snap on comb clip from the point where the neck meets the shoulder to the base of the tail. Make another stroke on each side of the first to widen the area. The rest of the clipped area of the body will be done with the clipper blade pointing straight down to the table. This blends the clipped area of the body into the skirt. Continue clipping straight down the sides to form a skirt making sure not to go under the body. Neaten the skirt with thinning shears.

Legs & Feet: Neaten the hocks with thinning shears. With curved scissors round the feet. Pull the hair up from between the toes and with thinning shears trim them following the toes' contours. Continue by neatening the leg feathers and any straggly hair with thinning shears.

Head & Ears: Chewey's muzzle hair is naturally short. Use thinning shears to trim the top of the head from shorter back to a longer neat stand up hair between the ears so it can be blended back into the "ruff ". Leave the "ruff's" length, neatening it with thinning shears and blending it into the shoulders. With straight scissors, scissor the ears to the leather and scissor the ear tops rounding them as much as possible.

Tail: Shape the tail into a carrot shape with thinning shears in proportion with the body approximately 1" at the base.

Alexa

Alexa is by far my favorite "wild woman." I'm really fortunate her dad usually just lets me thin her out a lot and leave this wild and wooly look. Not only does it look cool but it is so "her!"

Breeds that Alexa Most Resembles

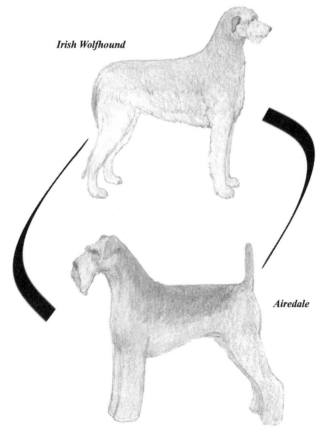

Irish Wolfhound

Airedale

ALEXA'S
First Visit Evaluation Notes

Outstanding features:
coloring
'wild look'
friendly & appealing eyes

Features to underplay:
overweight
'windmill ears'

Colors in coat:
cream
golden with black highlights

Coat texture:
dense undercoat
coarse
scruffy

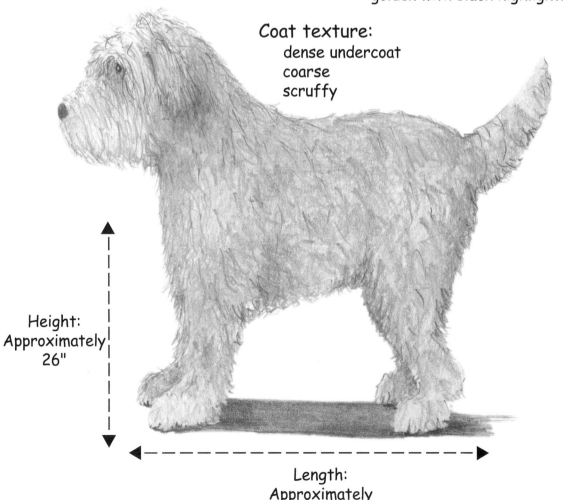

Height:
Approximately
26"

Length:
Approximately
33"

Makeover #53
Alexa as an Undercover Otterhound

Equipment:
- Slicker Brush
- V Rake
- Comb
- Clipper
- #10 Blade
- #40 Blade to use with the
- #1" Snap on Comb
- #1-1/4" Snap on Comb
- Thinning Shears
- Curved Scissor
- Straight Scissor
- Nail Trimmer

Alexa is approximately 26" tall, coarse and scruffy, natural, cream and golden with black highlighting. Sounds just like an Otterhound to me. What could be easier?

Body: Using a #1" snap on comb clip from the base of the neck to the base of the tail and all around the body.

Legs & Feet: Using a #1¼" snap on comb clip down the legs, picking up each leg and clipping over the foot. Round the feet with curved scissors.

continued...

Makeover #53
Alexa as an Undercover
Otterhound—cont'd.

Head & Ears: Trim the inside eye corners with thinning shears. Continue clipping with the #1¼" snap on comb on top of the head and sides of the face. Blend the base of the skull into the neck with thinning shears.

Tail: With thinning shears, shape the tail into a fox tail approximately 3" at the base.

Home Boy is my resident clown. The first time I talked with his Dad on the phone I asked what kind of a dog "Homey" was. As is often the case regarding mutts, he replied, "I don't know." Then I asked, "If you had to pick a breed that he looked the most like, which would it be?" He laughingly answered, "ugly!"

Home Boy

Breeds that Home Boy Most Resembles

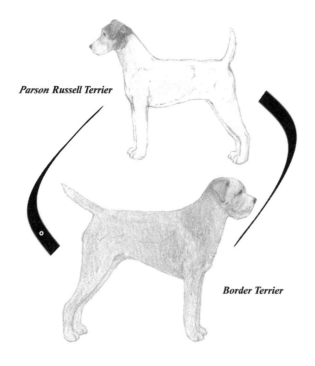

Parson Russell Terrier

Border Terrier

HOME BOY'S
First Visit Evaluation Notes

Features to underplay:
beard is sparse
wisps all over

Colors in coat:
golden
cream

Outstanding features:
comical playful attitude

Coat Texture:
very coarse guard hair
soft sparse undercoat

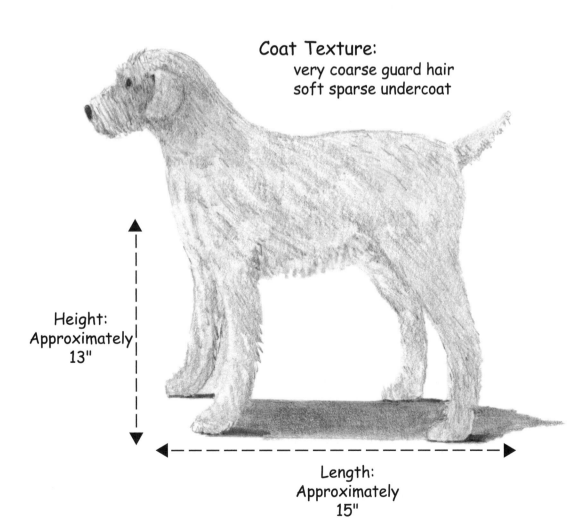

Height:
Approximately
13"

Length:
Approximately
15"

Makeover #54
Home Boy as a Border Terrier Puppy

Equipment:

- Slicker Brush
- Comb
- Clipper
- #10 Blade
- #40 Blade to use with the
- #3/8" (#2) Snap on Comb
- Curved Scissor
- Straight Scissor
- Nail Trimmer

Home Boy's personality can only be described as scruffy. Not only does he look the rough and tumble character, but he is one. We're going to give Home Boy a modified Border Terrier look that will calm some of his "wild man" look by taking about half of the long hair length off the body, legs, head, ears and tail. Then we will shape his face up like a Border Terrier.

Body: Using a #3/8" (#2) snap on comb clip from the base of the skull to the base of the tail and all around the body.

Legs & Feet: Continue clipping with the #3/8" (#2) snap on comb down the legs, picking up each leg and clipping over the foot. Round the feet with curved scissors.

Head & Ears: Using the #3/8" (#2) snap on comb clip the top of the head and ears leaving enough for a small visor. Scissor the ears to the leather's edge with straight scissors and curve the beard from the front to the outside eye corners with curved scissors and shape a short visor over the eyes.

Tail: Continue clipping with the #3/8" (#2) snap on comb all around the tail.

Makeover #55 Home Boy as a Miniature Spinone Italiano

Equipment:

- Slicker Brush
- Comb
- Clipper
- #10 Blade
- Thinning Shears
- Straight Scissor
- Nail Trimmer

Home Boy can successfully impersonate a Spinone. He's only half the usual size and though his color isn't exact, it's close. His shape is right and his coat texture matches too. You can't ask for more than that!

Body: Thin out if necessary by using thinning shears to make 2–3 cuts close to the skin and work out. Cut a small to medium section at a time. Remove any straggly hair with thinning shears. Neaten the skirt.

Legs & Feet: Leave the length, thin out if necessary. Round the feet with curved scissors.

Head & Ears: Scissor the inside eye corners and remove any straggly hair from the head with thinning shears. Scissor between the brows and triangulate them with straight scissors. Scissor the beard into a rectangular shape and neaten the ears with thinning shears.

Tail: Neaten the tail.

Makeover #56
Home Boy as an Irish Terrier

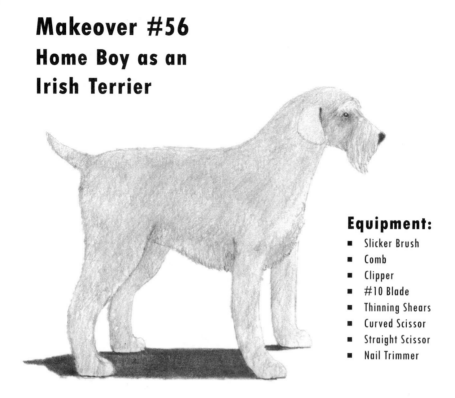

Equipment:
- Slicker Brush
- Comb
- Clipper
- #10 Blade
- Thinning Shears
- Curved Scissor
- Straight Scissor
- Nail Trimmer

Homeboy's size, shape and coat texture are so similar to an Irish Terrier's, let's see what he'd look like groomed as one.

Body: Using a #10 blade from the base of the skull to the base of the tail. Make another stroke on each side of the first to widen the area. The rest of the clipped area of the body will be done with the clipper blade pointing straight down to the table. This blends the clipped area of the body into the skirt. Continue clipping straight down the sides to leave a skirt. Do not go under the body. With thinning shears, trim the skirt very close following the body contours.

Legs & Feet: Continue clipping with the #10 blade down the back legs, clipping the back two-thirds of the leg halfway down to the hock. Scissor the rest of the leg short following its angles with curved scissors. With straight scissors pipe the front legs short. Round the feet with curved scissors.

Head & Ears: Using the #10 blade clip the top of the head leaving enough hair for eyebrows. Continue clipping down the sides of the face between the outer eye corners and underneath the ears. Using a #10 blade clip on both sides of the ears with straight scissors and triangulate the eyebrows short. Shape the beard into a long barrel shape with a small goatee with thinning shears.

Tail: Continue clipping with a #10 blade all around the tail.

Makeover #57
Home Boy as a German Wirehaired Pointer

Equipment:
- Slicker Brush
- Comb
- Clipper
- #10 Blade
- #4F Blade
- Thinning Shears
- Straight Scissor
- Nail Trimmer

Even though Home Boy is only half the size of a German Wirehaired Pointer and the wrong color, he has the right shape and coat texture to make this a successful look. I'm going to borrow the style and I'll just make him a mini.

Body: Using a #4F blade clip from the base of the skull to the base of the tail and all around the body.

Legs & Feet: Continue clipping with the #4F blade down the legs, picking up each leg and clipping over the foot. Round the feet with curved scissors.

Head & Ears: Using a #10 blade clip the top of the head and sides of the face between the outer eye corners and underneath the ears, leaving enough length for eyebrows and a beard. With straight scissors, scissor between the eyebrows then triangulate them. Clip the ears inside and out with the same blade. Neaten the edges of the ear leather with scissors, pointing the bottoms. Scissor the beard rectangular and short with thinning shears.

Tail: Using a #4F blade clip all around the tail.

Shelby & Jackson

Shelby and Jackson, A.K.A. "The Twins," are so full of vinegar! Energy like that should be bottled and sold. Their Mom keeps harnesses on them so she has a fighting chance of catching them when they are running around. Despite their non-stop energy, they are also bundles of joy in fur coats.

Breeds that Shelby & Jackson Most Resemble

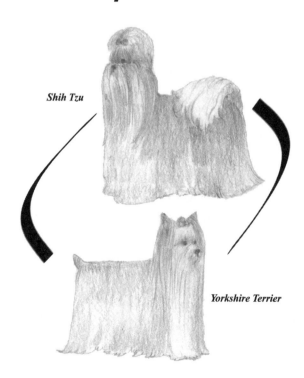

Shih Tzu

Yorkshire Terrier

SHELBY & JACKSON'S
First Visit Evaluation Notes

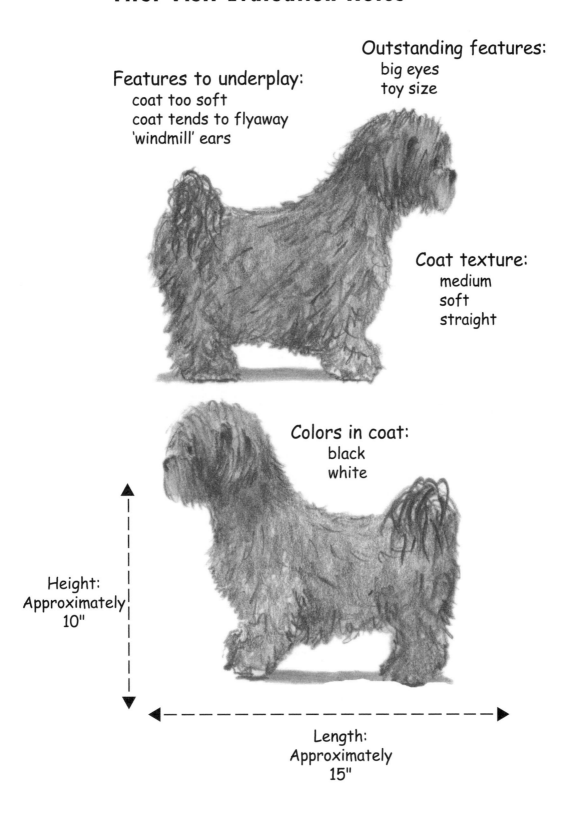

Features to underplay:
coat too soft
coat tends to flyaway
'windmill' ears

Outstanding features:
big eyes
toy size

Coat texture:
medium
soft
straight

Colors in coat:
black
white

Height:
Approximately
10"

Length:
Approximately
15"

Makeover #58
Jackson Sporting a Chinese Crested Hairless Look

Equipment:

- Comb
- Clipper
- #10 Blade
- #15 Blade
- Thinning Shears
- Curved Scissor
- Nail Trimmer

I'm going to try some real "mutt magic" on "The Twins." Their personality and high energy are somewhat comical and remind me of the Chinese Crested Dog. Why not take advantage of their small size, "windmill ears," and color since Chinese Cresteds can be all colors and combinations. This is creativity at its peak!!!

Body: Lift the hair and using a #15 blade start clipping where the neck connects to the body. Leave the mane natural. Clip to the base of the tail. Clip all around the body lifting the hair so it can flow halfway over the shoulder.

Legs & Feet: Continue clipping with the #15 blade down the legs to just above the hock joints and the wrists, leaving the rest (socks) intact and flowing. Making them equal in size. Round the feet with curved scissors.

Head & Ears: Using a #15 blade clip the muzzle clean and continue back to inside the ear. Clip down the throat holding the mane up so it can flow naturally. Form an inverted "V" at the stop. Leave the length on the top of the head and comb it back. Allow the hair on the ears to be long and flowing, neatening with thinning shears if necessary.

Tail: Using a #15 blade clip all around the tail two-thirds of the way down leaving a plume on the end. Neaten with thinning shears if necessary.

Makeover #59
Shelby as a Chinese Crested Powder Puff

Equipment:

- Slicker Brush
- Pin Brush
- Comb
- Clipper
- #10 Blade and/or
- #15 Blade
- Thinning Shears
- Curved Scissor
- Nail Trimmer

If Jackson can be a Chinese Crested why can't his twin, Shelby? But let's not make them totally the same. Why not try to create a Powder Puff? I'm going to take advantage of two things. "The Twins" have Shih Tzu and Yorkshire Terrier in their background, the perfect coat types for this full coated style. Again, their "windmill ears" will be almost perfect in this style as they are the next best thing to stand up ears.

Body: Leaving the length, thin out if necessary by using thinning shears to make 2–3 cuts, starting close to the skin and work out. Cut a small to medium section at a time. Part the coat from the base of the skull to the base of the tail. Neaten with thinning shears.

Legs & Feet: Leave the length and if necessary thin out. Neaten with thinning shears. Round the feet to be large and full with curved scissors.

Head & Ears: Using a #15 blade clip the muzzle clean, using the outside eye corners as the pattern. Form an inverted "V" at the stop. Clip down the throat to the Adam's apple to form a "U" or "necklace." Leave the length on top of the head and comb it back. Allow the hair on the ears to be long and flowing, neatening with thinning shears.

Tail: Leave the length, neatening with thinning shears.

Sam

I just adore Sam! I've nicknamed him my "Little Joe," because his body, coat texture and eyes are so like my Joseph's.

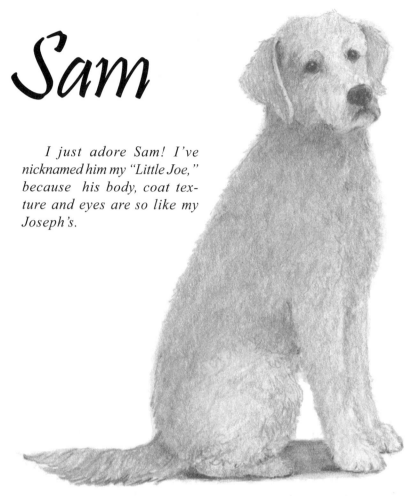

Breeds that Sam Most Resembles

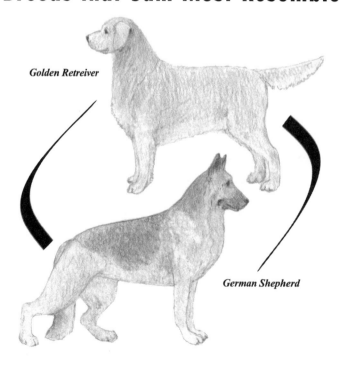

Golden Retreiver

German Shepherd

SAM'S
First Visit Evaluation Notes

Outstanding features:
soft expressive eyes
friendliness
rich color

Features to underplay:
none

Colors in coat:
red
brown
black

Coat texture:
medium coarse guard hair
soft undercoat

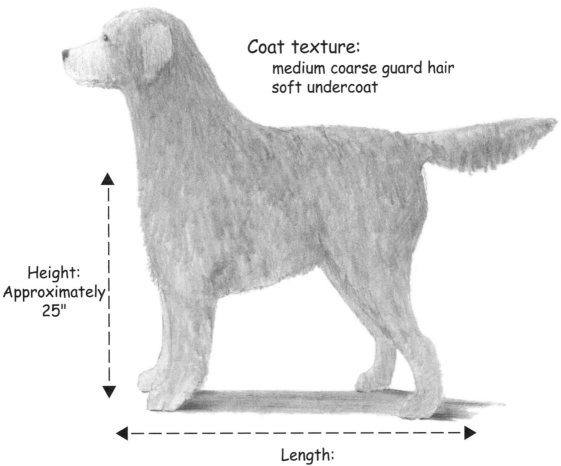

Height:
Approximately
25"

Length:
Approximately
32"

Makeover #60
Sam the Puppy

Equipment:

- Slicker Brush
- Comb
- Clipper
- #10 Blade
- #40 Blade to use with the
- #1 Snap on Comb
- Thinning Shears
- Curved Scissor
- Straight Scissor
- Nail Trimmer

All we have to do is shorten Sam up and fluff him out. This will make him easy to care for as well as give him a different look.

Body: Using a #1 snap on comb clip from the base of the skull to the base of the tail and all around the body. Another way to achieve this is to use your #10 blade and skim the aforementioned area. A clipper vacuuming system helps make this technique much easier and faster. Use thinning shears to blend in any mishaps.

Legs & Feet: Use the same shortening technique down the legs and flanks. Using thinning shears, shorten the front leg feathers to be proportionate with the rest of the body. Trim the bottoms of the feet with straight scissors. Pull the hair up from between the toes and following the contours of the toe hair, scissor them with thinning shears, trying not to expose the nails. Clean the pasterns and the hocks with straight scissors or thinning shears.

Tail: Shorten the underside of the tail with thinning shears to approximately 4½– 5" keeping it in proportion to the body.

Note: "Skim:" To shorten and sculpt hair length with the clippers instead of scissors (free hand).

Makeover #61
Sam as a Golden Retriever

Equipment:
- Slicker Brush
- Shedding Blade
- Comb
- Clipper
- #10 Blade
- #7F Blade
- #4 Skip Tooth Blade
- Thinning Shears
- Straight Scissor
- Nail Trimmer

I decided that with some shaping, we could bring out the Golden Retriever genes in Sam. He has the coat to grow out so now it's our job to sculpt it.

Body: Using a #4 skip tooth blade clip from the base of the skull to the base of the tail. Make another stroke on each side of the first to widen the area. The rest of the clipped area of the body will be done with the blade pointing straight down to the table. This blends the clipped area of the body into the skirt. Continue clipping straight down the sides creating a long skirt. Do not go under the body. Blend and neaten with thinning shears where necessary.

Legs & Feet: Using a #7F blade clip on the front and sides of the front legs from the top and picking up each leg continue clipping over the foot. On the back legs follow the stifle with thinning shears leaving approximately ¾". Where the stifle curve ends and the leg straightens, continue clipping with a #7F blade straight down on the front and two sides. Pick up each leg and clip over the foot. With thinning shears, neaten the hocks, pasterns, and top of foot following the contours of the toes. Round the feet with curved scissors.

Head & Ears: Using a #10 blade clip the top of the head and the face and blend into the neck making sure not to go under the neck. Comb the long ear feathers toward the back of the ear and shorten them to the leather using thinning shears. Repeat this process combing the feathers to the front of the ear. Comb the shortened feathers straight down and neaten them with thinning shears until the ear looks neat but natural.

Tail: Neaten with thinning shears.

Bailey

Last but not least is Bailey. I met Bailey when he was a tiny puppy, only weeks old. He looks like a tiny stuffed toy and is just as huggable!

Breeds that Bailey Most Resembles

Toy Poodle

Lhasa Apso

BAILEY'S
First Visit Evaluation Notes

Outstanding features:
touchable coat
monkey-like face
big eyes

Features to underplay:
long body
long feet

Colors in coat:
cream

Coat texture:
wavy
soft

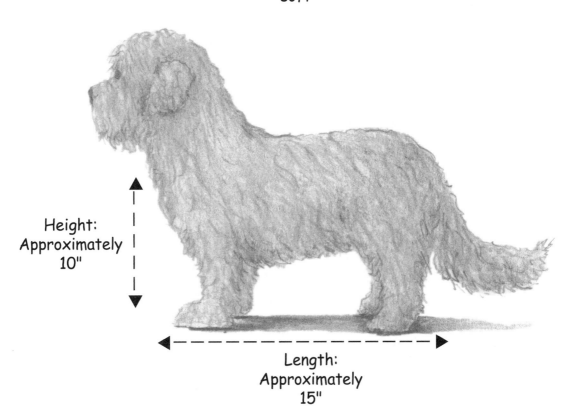

Height:
Approximately
10"

Length:
Approximately
15"

Makeover #62
Bailey as a Lhasa Puppy

Equipment:

- Slicker Brush
- Comb
- Clipper
- #10 Blade
- #40 Blade to use with the
- #1¼" Snap on Comb
- Thinning Shears
- Curved Scissor
- Straight Scissor
- Nail Trimmer

Bailey is such a cute puppy and will make a perfect looking Lhasa Apso. With the exception of Bailey's coat being a little softer and an almost cartoonish, monkey-like look on his face, Bailey doesn't have any "mutt issues." Everything else is perfect.

Body: Using a #1¼" snap on comb clip from the base of the skull to the base of the tail and all around the body.

Legs & Feet: Scissor the legs full and piped with straight scissors. Round the feet to be large and fluffy with curved scissors.

Head & Ears: Trim the inside eye corners with straight scissors. Comb from the base of the skull forward and trim in front of the eyes and down the sides of the face with curved scissors. Continue by shortening the ears, and beveling the bottoms into the circle. Fluff the top of the head and round into the full circle with the curved scissors.

Tail: Trim the underside of the tail with thinning shears to approximately 4½–5" long.

Makeover #63
Bailey All Grown Up

Equipment:

- Slicker Brush
- Comb
- Clipper
- #10 Blade
- Thinning Shears
- Straight Scissor
- Nail Trimmer

If we can make Bailey a Lhasa Apso puppy, why can't we make him into an adult in full coat? We can take Bailey from a puppy to a grown up by growing his coat out and changing his entire look.

Body: Leaving the length, thin out if necessary by using thinning shears make 2–3 cuts close to the skin and work out. Cut a small to medium section at a time. Part the coat from the base of the skull to the base of the tail.

Legs & Feet: Leaving the length, thin out if necessary. Round the feet with curved scissors.

Head & Ears: Scissor the inside eye corners with straight scissors. Part down the center of the top of the head. **Note**: You also have the option to put a topknot, pigtails or nubs on the head (refer to page 52).

Tail: Leave the length and neaten with thinning shears.

Makeover #64
Bailey Looks Great as a Brussels Griffon

Equipment:

- Slicker Brush
- Comb
- Clipper
- #10 Blade
- #40 Blade to use with the
- #3/8" (#2) Snap on Comb
- Thinning Shears
- Curved Scissor
- Straight Scissor
- Nail Trimmer

One way to enhance Bailey's big eyes is to make him into a Brussels Griffon. We'll modify his body by leaving a skirt that will give his brisket and loin tuck up the appearance of being lower, breaking up Bailey's length a little. We'll pipe his legs and last but not least, we'll trim his tail close.

Body: Using a #3/8" (#2) snap on comb clip from the base of the skull to the base of the tail. Make another stroke on each side of the first to widen the area. The rest of the clipped area of the body will be done with the snap on comb pointing straight down to the table. This blends the clipped area of the body into the skirt. Continue clipping straight down the sides making sure not to go under the body. Scissor the brisket longer and then angle it sharply up to the loin tuck up with thinning shears.

Legs & Feet: With straight scissors, pipe the front and the back legs to approximately 1½–2" long. Round the feet and bevel them with curved scissors.

Head & Ears: Using a #5F blade clip the top of the head and straight—do not go under—down the sides of the face between the outer eye corner and underneath the ear leaving beneath the clipped area as the beard. Scissor the beard so it looks rounded but the length remains full. Fluff the beard out but not forward. Using a #10 blade clip on both sides of the ears and scissor them to the leather to neaten with thinning shears.

Tail: Trim the underside of the tail with thinning shears to approximately 3½–4".

Appendix

Glossary & Suggested Reading

a

Accent: The groomer draws attention to an attractive feature on the dog with the style chosen.

"Accent the Brisket:" The groomer makes the dog's brisket appear deeper (longer) by scissoring this hair as long as proportionately possible and the loin tuck-up as short as proportionately possible.

Adam's Apple: The bulge in the front of the dog's neck.

Aggressive Behavior: A dog showing signs of hostile actions.

Alternative Style: A different hair cut for a dog.

Angles: The contours of the dog's body.

Angulated Legs: While shaping the dog's legs, the groomer follows its contours.

Apprenticing: Learning to groom dogs through on the job training while gaining practical experience.

b

Bandy Legs: An outward bend of the rear legs causing a wider appearance in the rear of the dog.

Bangs: A fringe of hair over the dog's eyes, also referred to as a visor.

Base of the Skull: The back of the dog's head where it connects to the neck.

Base of the Tail: The point of a dog's tail where it connects to the body.

Bell Bottom: A leg style in which the hair on the leg flares out at the foot.

Bent Shank Scissors: Scissors where the finger holes are offset from the line of the blades achieved by putting a bend in the shank. The offset angle helps to ease wrist fatigue and comes in varying lengths usually between 8¼–10".

Bevel: To taper or angle the bottom edge inward.

Blend: The smooth and precise transition between two differing lengths of hair. It is usually achieved using thinning shears, a skip tooth clipper blade, or a snap on comb. Blending eliminates the "shelf" or "hula skirt" look.

Blowing Coat: The natural process in which the dog's coat rejuvenates itself and dead hair falls out. This occurs according to the dog's body, not necessarily due to seasonal changes throughout the year.

Body Contours: The angles of the dog's body.

Bodylines: The different contours of a dog's shape.

"Bottom of the Tail:" As referred to with the Bedlington Terrier tail (page 85) is the section of the circumference of the tail nearest the tip.

Bows: Loop approximately 4" of ribbon. Take the center of the loop at the top and pinch it down behind the crossover. Wrap a small latex band around the center pinched section 4-6 times. Be as creative as you wish by adding nylon net, ribbon roses, another bow, streamers, etc.

Bracelets: The rounded balls of hair on the ankles of some Poodle styles.

Brisket: The part of the dog's chest on the underside. Also referred to as the sternum and the underchest.

Build Up: Filling in an indented area of the dog's body with hair to make it appear normal or straight.

Butterfly Look: A dog with ears that stand up and have long flowing hair growing out from the sides as seen on the Papillon on page 56.

C

Carding: Removing dead hair and undercoat.

Carpus: A dog's wrists.

Caution Dog: Warning! This can be an aggressive dog.

Chippendale Front: A dog with a combination of: out at the elbow, pasterns that are too close and feet that turn out. **Note**: Also called a Fiddle Front.

Clipper Vacuuming System: A tool that attaches to clippers and sucks up the cut coat into a container as the groomer is clipping the dog.

Coat Texture: The structure, feel and appearance of the outer hair covering of a dog.

Cockapoo: The crossbreeding of the Cocker Spaniel and the Poodle. The name Cockapoo has also in recent years become a generic term for many mixed breeds.

Cow-Hocked: Dog hocks that point inward while the rear feet toe outward.

Crest: The curved upper portion of the dog's neck.

Cross Breeds: Dogs that are a mixture of two separate pure breeds.

Crown: The hair on the front of the dog's topskull from the eyebrows back approximately ¼ of the skull length. This hair is blended into the rest of the skull with thinning shears to give the head a more squared off appearance. See the American Cocker Spaniel.

Cuff: An untrimmed bracelet as seen on the Lowchen.

Curved Scissors: Scissors that have cutting blades that arch. These expedite the scissoring of topknots, the tops of pantaloons, pompons, and bracelets because the blades more closely follow the natural curvature of these parts. Curved scissors come in various lengths usually from 4–10".

Cylindrical Shape: A long round form, usually styled onto legs and beards.

Dematting: To manually remove tight knots and large mats from a dog's coat.

Dethatching: Removing dead hair and undercoat from a dog's body.

Digits: The dog's toes.

Do Not Go Under The Body: This is in reference to the clippers being used straight down the dog's sides only. Do not shave, just neaten the underside with scissors.

Donut: A small round moustache that continues to circle under the chin too. It should be kept close to the nose and away from the corners of the mouth.

Down in Pastern: A condition where the dog has a weak metacarpus (pastern) angled incorrectly backwards.

e

Ear Canal: The tubular passage in the dog's ear.

Elongate: To give the illusion on a dog's body of extra length.

Ergonomic Equipment: Tools specially designed to reduce stress on the groomer's body, minimize effort, and promote comfort.

f

Fall: The dog's hair above the eyebrows, which hangs over the eyes and face. When grooming, do not scissor out between the eyes. **Note**: Airedale, Kerry Blue Terrier and Soft Coated Wheaten Terriers all have falls.

Feathering: The longer decorative hair on a dog's ears, body, legs or tail, also referred to as Furnishings or Fringe.

Features: The parts of the dog that are especially noticeable or characteristic.

Fiddle Front: A dog with a combination of; out at the elbow, pasterns that are too close and feet that turn out. **Note**: Also called a Chippendale Front.

Field Clip: The clipped "U" shape on the thighs, exposing the upper thigh muscle, for an example see the English Springer Spaniel.

Finishing Clipper Blades: Clipper blades (i.e. 5F, 7F) with regular length teeth. These make a smoother, more even cut needed for the final grooming.

Flare: A dog's coat spreading outward away from the body. Also referred to as a Bell Bottom.

Flew: The hanging part of a dog's upper lip.

Fluff Up: The groomer making the dog's coat stand up and out.

Flyaways: Wisps of hair sticking out that are longer than the rest. It's noticeable because it doesn't look right standing out from the rest. They are also referred to as Wisps.

Focal Point: The main thing you see when looking at the dog.

Fox Tail: A dog's tail, pointed at the tip, widening out at the center and widening more at the base.

Framing the Eyes: Emphasizing a dog's eyes by trimming back the hair covering them.

Free Hand: To shorten the dog's coat without any mechanical devices to premeasure the length.

Fringe: The longer decorative hair on a dog's ears, body, legs or tail. Also referred to as Furnishings or Feathering.

Fritz: A grooming style where the head and ears are styled as a Border Terrier, the body and legs as a Schnauzer with a fox tail.

From the Elbow to Just Below the Rectum: A part of the pattern for dog styles describing the clipper line the body is brought down to on the sides.

Full Coat: A dog's coat allowed to grow into its natural length.

Furnishings: The longer decorative hair on a dog's ears, body, legs and tail. Also referred to as Feathering or Fringe.

g

Grain: The natural direction of hair growth in the dog's coat. Brushing, combing, clipping or cutting in the same direction as the hair growth is referred to as "with the grain." Brushing, combing, clipping or cutting in the opposite direction of hair growth is referred to as "against the grain."

Groin: The dog's genital area. **Note**: This area needs to be checked and cleaned at each visit.

Grooming School: An establishment teaching the art of styling and grooming dogs.

Guard Hair: The dog's coarse topcoat.

h

Hairmostats®: A tool specially designed for easily removing the hair from dogs' ears. Similar to a hemostat, but more specialized, for the grooming industry with non-slip vinyl handles and no locking clamp to interfere with its use. It is also used for removing ticks.

Heart-Shaped Ears: A dog's ear leather shaped like a heart with the point at the bottom.

Height: The height of a dog is measured from the floor to the withers.

Hemostats: A tool that resembles scissors with handles that lock into a closed position. They are used in dog grooming to extract hair from a dog's ear, put bows in, remove ticks and splinters, etc. Sometimes they are referred to as Kelly Foreceps.

Highlights: Different colored hair sporadically interjected thoughout the coat that emphasizes the dominant color.

Hock: The dog's heel. The group of bones of the back leg shaping the joint between the lower thigh and the metatarsus.

Hock Joint: The joint on the dog's back leg found between the lower thigh and the rear pastern.

Hound Glove: Brush bristles embedded in a glove or mitt. It helps bring out the shine in the dog's coat.

Hula Skirt: The line left on a dog after grooming around the lower part of the torso. Because it is two different distinct hair lengths, the lower part sticks out giving the dog an unnatural look.

Hydraulic Grooming Tables: Tables using hydraulic power to raise and lower them, usually from 19–41". There are electrically powered tables too. These tables eliminate the stress from lifting the dog for both the groomer and the dog. They usually hold up to 300 lbs.

i

Illusion: The stylist covering up unattractive features on the dog with creative and different styling that makes the dog more attractive.

Incorporate: The groomer merges or blends two lengths of a dog's coat giving it a smooth appearance.

k

Knobby Head: Rounded lumps or protuberances on the top of a dog's skull.

Knuckled Over: A dog that has wrists that bend forward while it is standing straight.

l

Leather: The flap of the dog's ear.

Leg Extensions: These increase the regular height of a grooming table to create an adjusted custom extension.

Length: The length of the dog is measured from the front of the chest to the back of the rump.

Lion Cut: The grooming style that has a natural full front (approximately two-thirds of the body) with the back one-third of the body shaved down, leaving a plume on the end of the tail. There are different variations to this style.

Loin: The part of the dog's body on each side of its spinal column, between the hip and lower ribs.

Loin Tuck-Up: The point of a dog's underside in front of the back legs where the body draws up.

m

Maintenance: The upkeep and care of a dog's coat in between groomings.

Markings: The specific areas of different color on a dog.

Mats: A tangled mass of dog hair.

Metacarpus: The dog's front pastern.

Metatarsis: The dog's rear pastern.

Mixed Breeds: Dogs with more than two different breeds in them.

Modified: To adapt or change a style.

Mutt: Short for "mutton head." Now referring to mixed breed dogs.

Mutt Issues: Referring to the conditions present in a mutt preventing it from looking as close as it can to a pure bred dog. These issues include coat type and texture, physical deformaties, and problems with proprtions. These issues can usually be remedied or hidden by the use of Mutt Magic.

Mutt Magic: The ability of the groomer to determine which breeds may be within a mutt's genetic mix and to identify physical imperfections. Then through the mixing and matching of different grooming techniques and styles and hiding those physical imperfections, creates an "illusion," (unique styling) that makes the finished mutt as attractive as possible.

n

Nail Trimmers: A tool used to shorten a dog's toenails. There are a variety of types: The scissors-type for small nails, the guillotine-type for medium sized nails, and the pliers-type which are found in assorted sizes. Pliers-type trimmers are more versatile because they are open on the end.

Narrow Front: A dog's front legs that are too close together. They also have a slender chest.

Narrow Rear: A dog's back legs that are too close together.

Natural: Having the dog's look remain normal and true to the breed.

Neaten: To tidy up an area on the dog by evening, straightening, clipping and/or thinning out.

Necklace: Clip down the dog's neck from the muzzle. Using the outside corner of the ear as a starting point, continue to clip down the throat to the Adam's apple in the shape of a "U" or a "V."

Nub: Twist and fold over a dog's pigtail or top knot into a small projecting part. See page 52.

o

Occiput: The back part of the dog's head or skull.

Offset: To counterbalance or make up for any disproportionate body parts.

Out at the Elbow: Elbows on the dog that point out.

Outermost Point: The spot located the farthest out.

Overflowing Topknot: A dog's topknot that extends a little over the skull, eyes and ear tops as in the Dandie Dinmont Terrier, on page 57.

Overshot Jaw: The space between the dog's front upper and lower teeth created by the upper front teeth protruding beyond the lower.

Oversized Ears: A dog's ears that are too large in proportion to its body.

P

3 P's: Proportion, Proportion, Proportion. This is to remind the groomer to always keep in mind that no matter how good the job is, if some part of the body looks too big or too small, you did not accomplish your objective.

Pantaloons: A dog's leg style that continues up the leg and onto the body in an inverted "U" shape. Its length is longer than the body's coat length to make it stand out (refer to page 74).

Pastern: The area of the dog's legs between the wrist and the toes Also referred to as the Metacarpus and Metatarsus.

Pattern: The model or design after which a dog's coat is formed.

Pee Bee-Gee Vee: (PBGV) The abbreviations for the Petit Basset Griffon Vendeen.

Pet Clips: The type of styling groomers create for dogs not in competition.

PH-Balance:

Acidity					Neutrality						Alkalinity		
1	2	3	4	5	6	7	8	9	10	11	12	13	14

PH-BALANCE SCALE

Note: Do not use shampoo made for people unless recommended by a veterinarian. Use only dog shampoo because the PH-Balance is different.

Pigtails: Part off two sections of hair evenly on top of the dog's head and wrap latex bands around each 2–3 times to form pigtails.

Pin Brush: Shaped with a handle similar to a woman's wig brush but with pins placed in rubber backing and spread out farther apart than a slicker brush. Used to protect long flowing coats.

Piped Legs: Scissoring the dog's legs into a cylindrical shape. For an example refer to page 73.

Plucking Ears: Removing the hair from a dog's ear to allow air to get into it. This helps to keep the ear free from bacteria and the possibility of infection.

Plume: The remaining hair feathering left on the dog's tail.

Plumed Tail: A tail style where the tail feathering is left long and flowing.

Points of Reference: Area on a dog's body used for setting a pattern for a style.

Pompons: The rounded balls of hair on the tail and/or ankles of some poodle cuts.

Ponytail: Part off a section of hair evenly on the top of the dog's head and wrap a latex band around it 2–3 times. Also called a topknot.

Poodle Feet: Feet that are totally shaved including between the toes and the pads, and are shaved up to the wrist.

Poodle Tail: The rounded ball of hair on the end of a poodle tail, also called a pompon.

Puppy Cut: The same length of coat on a dog's body and legs. There is no specific length required and it can be varied from dog to dog. Just be sure that the body length and leg length remains uniform. **Note**: All puppy cuts referred to in this book are for the pet, not the show dog.

Pure Breeds: Dogs of a recognized breed without a mixture of other bloodlines over a span of many generations.

PWD: The abbreviation for the Portuguese Water Dog.

r

Rat Tail: A dog's tail style in which the top third has some coat and the bottom two-thirds is shaved as seen on the Bedlington, Irish Water Spaniel.

Rectum: The area of the dog's body under the tail and around the anus. **Note**: This area needs to be checked and cleaned at each visit.

S

Schnuppy: A grooming style where the head and ears are made to look like a Schnauzer and the body, legs and tail are put into a Puppy Cut.

Scruffy: A dog with an untidy, unkempt appearance.

Sculpt: To fashion a dog's coat with precision and artistry.

SCW: The abbreviation for Soft Coated Wheaten Terrier.

Shallow Stop: The area located on the dog, where the muzzle meets the skull between the eyes, lacking depth as seen on the Collie.

Shape: Forming a particular pattern or look on the dog.

Shed: Natures way of eliminating the dog's dead hair from its coat.

Shedding Blade: A tool used to remove dead hair and undercoat, also referred to as Carding.

Shelf: The distinct line of different hair lengths left when grooming the dog, giving the dog an unnatural looking hula skirt.

Show Clips: The styles put on dogs being shown in competition.

Skim: Free-hand shaping of the upper portion of the dog's coat with clippers.

Skip Tooth Clipper Blades: Clipper blades with irregular lengths of teeth. These are best used to clip under matting, rough cuts and blending.

Slew Feet: A dog's feet that turn out and away from the body.

Slicker Brush: A tool with angled wire teeth placed in a soft pad with a handle. It is used to untangle and remove dead hair and mats.

Snap on Combs: Varying sized combs that attach onto clipper blades achieving longer lengths of hair, different from the regular blade lengths.

Socks: The hair left on a Chinese Crested's ankles and wrists.

Stifle: The dog's knee.

Stop: The area located on the dog where the muzzle meets the skull between the eyes.

Straight Scissors: Scissors that have uncurved blades and come in various lengths usually from 4–10".

Stripping Knife: A tool with a serrated edge used to strip, pluck or remove dead hair and undercoat. A procedure sometimes referred to as carding.

Stroke: A single unbroken motion with the clippers.

Stylist: One who fashions, designs and styles a dog's coat to make them appear more attractive and leave them feeling better.

Taper: To make the hair gradually shorter toward one end.

Tarsus: The dog's heel.

Tassel: The fringe hair on the tip of Bedlington Terrier and Dandie Dinmont Terrier ears.

Techniques: Grooming methods used to accomplish the desired goal, whether it be scissoring, skimming a coat with clippers, dematting or shaving.

Thin Out: A technique that not only shortens the coat a little but also relieves the coat of a lot of its thickness by using thinning shears. Make 2–3 cuts starting close to the skin, working out and cutting only a small to medium section of hair at a time.

Thinning Shears: Scissors with varying number of teeth, usually between 30–46 teeth, in one blade or both blades and come in varying lengths usually between 5–7½". They can be used for blending, thinning out and giving the coat a natural look while finishing.

Toothpick Legs: One of the names that is not a technical term yet, but needs to be. The dog's legs are too long and thin for the body. They look like toothpicks were set under a large body to hold it up.

Topknot: The small pony tail as seen on the Yorkshire Terrier.

Triangulate Brows: To scissor the eyebrows shorter from the outside eye corner, graduating to a longer point toward the inside eye corner.

Trim the Clipped Edges: Scissoring the borders of the clipped areas to straighten and tidy, for example see Cocker Spaniel ears on page (67).

Tuft: A small bunch of long hair and an outgrowth of hair on a dog.

u

Undercoat: The soft, short, down-like coat close to the dog's skin lying under the topcoat or guard hairs.

Undershot Jaw: The dog's front teeth of the lower jaw protruding over the upper jaw's front teeth when the mouth is in a closed position.

Utility Do: A dog's haircut that serves primarily for usefulness rather than beauty. It is usually a shavedown or very short clip.

V

Variations: To change part of a dog's style, changing the look.

Visor: A fringe of hair hanging over the dog's eyes, also referred to as Bangs.

V RAKE®: Grooming tool used for dematting that does not destroy the coat. Never use a jerking stroke or ripping stroke, always use a short picking motion to remove the mats.

W

Wee Kerry: A grooming style where the head and ears are made to look like a Kerry Blue Terrier, the body and legs like a Soft Coated Wheaten Terrier and the tail trimmed to proportion.

Wide Front: A dog's front legs having a large leg spread and a broad chest.

Wide Rear Stance: A dog having back legs that naturally stand too far apart.

Windmill Ears: The name I've given to a dog's ears that should normally hang down but the leather is too short so instead they stick out horizontally from the head.

Wisps: Small and thin quantities of hair sticking out and are longer than the rest. They are so noticeable because they don't look right standing out where they are.

Withers: The ridge between the shoulder bones of the dog.

Suggested Reading

All About Dog Shows, Sam Kohl, Aaronco Pet Products, Inc., Hicksville, NY.

All Breed Dog Grooming Guide, Sam Kohl, Aaronco Pet Products, Inc., Hicksville, NY.

The Atlas of Dog Breeds of the World, Bonnie Wilcox, DVM. and Chris Walkowicz. T.F.H. Publications, Inc., Neptune City, NJ. 1989.

The Complete Dog Book, The Official Publication of AKS, Howell House, New York, NY.

Dogs, Desmond Morris, Trafalgar Square Publishing, North Pomfret, Vermont.

Dog, Juliet Glutton-Brock, Dorling Kindersley Publishing, Inc., New York, NY.

Dog Facts, Joan Palmer, Quantum Books, London, England, Barnes & Noble, Inc.

The Encyclopedia of Dog Breeds, Parragon, Barnes & Noble, Inc.

Illustrated Dog Watching, Desmond Morris, Cresent Books, Avenel, NJ.

The Secret Lives of Dogs, Jane Murphy & The Editors of Pets, Rodale Books.

ASPCA Complete Guide to Dogs, Sheldon L. Gerstenfeld, V.M.D., with Jacque Lynn Schultz, San Francisco, CA.

Notes

Notes

Notes

Notes

Notes